Landscapes of
FUERTEVENTURA
a countryside guide
Eighth edition

Noel Rochford
revised by Sunflower Books
with Conny Spelbrink and Jan Kostura

SUNFLOWER BOOKS

Eighth edition © 2025
Sunflower Books™
PO Box 36160
London SW7 3WS, UK
www.sunflowerbooks.co.uk

All rights reserved. No part of this publication may be reproduced, stored in a retrieval system, or transmitted in any form or by any means, electronic, mechanical, photocopying, recording or otherwise, without the prior written permission of the publishers.

Sunflower Books and 'Landscapes' are Registered Trademarks.

ISBN 978-1-85691-560-1

Molino de El Roque (Walk 6)

Important note to the reader

We have tried to ensure that the descriptions and maps in this book are error-free at press date. It is very helpful for us to receive your comments (sent to info@sunflowerbooks.co.uk, please) for the updating of future editions.

We also rely on those who use this book — especially walkers — to take along a good supply of common sense when they explore. Conditions change fairly rapidly on Fuerteventura, and ***storm damage or bulldozing may make a route unsafe at any time***. If the route is not as we outline it here, and your way ahead is not secure, return to the point of departure. ***Never attempt to complete a tour or walk under hazardous conditions!*** Please read the Country code on page 15 and the notes on pages 37 to 43, as well as the introductory comments at the beginning of each tour and walk (about road conditions, equipment, grade, distances and time, etc). Explore *safely*, while at the same time respecting the beauty of the countryside.

Cover photo: Playa de Cofete
Title page: welcome to Pájara!

Photos on pages 17, 18-9, 20-1, 22, 24 (all), 26-7, 36 (top), 44-5, 51, 53, 56, 58-9, 60-1, 70-1, 72 (foot), 84 (both), 90, 92, 100 (foot), 103, 117, 118-9, 121 (right, centre and foot), 128 (top left), 128-9: Jan Kostura; 1, 2, 37, 57, 63 (foot), 72 (top), 74, 80-1, 82 (left), 101, 109, 110-1, 121 (right, top): Robert Lefever; 13, 36, 50-1, 52, 55, 61, 75 (top), 77, 88-9, 94-5, 96, 97, 100 (top), 106-7, 114-5, 121 (top left), 129 (all), 130, 132-3, 135, 136 (all), 144-5, 147, 148: Noel Rochford; 29, 31, 32-3, 46-7, 54, 78-9, 96-7, 104-5, 108, 124-5, 138-9, cover: Shutterstock; 4, 12, 15, 26-7, 28 (both), 40, 41, 48, 63 (top two), 67 (both), 82 (right), 86-7, 91: Conny Spelbrink; 17, 35, 38-9, 140-1, 148, 149: John Underwood
Maps: Nick Hill for Sunflower Books. Base map data © OpenStreetMap contributors. Contour data made available under ODbL (opendatacommons.org/licenses/odbl/1.0)
A CIP catalogue record for this book is available from the British Library.
Printed and bound in England: Short Run Press, Exeter

Contents

Preface	5
Acknowledgements; Useful books	6
Town plans	6-10
Morro Jable (6), Caleta de Fuste (7), Puerto del Rosario (8-9), Gran Tarajal (9), Corralejo (10)	
Getting about	7
Picnics and short walks	11
Picnic suggestions	11
Touring	14
A country code for walkers and motorists	15
Car tour 1: THE BEST OF FUERTEVENTURA	16
Morro Jable • La Pared • Pájara • Betancuria • Antigua • Gran Tarajal • Las Playitas • Morro Jable	
Car tour 2: PUNTA DE JANDIA AND THE WEST COAST	25
Morro Jable • Punta de Jandía • Cofete • Morro Jable	
Car tour 3: NORTHERN LANDSCAPES	30
Corralejo • Puerto del Rosario • Tetir • Tefía • Los Molinos • Tindaya • Vallebrón • La Oliva • El Cotillo • Corralejo	
Walking (● see explanation of symbols on page 37)	37
Grading, waymarking, maps, GPS	37
Where to stay	38
What to take	39
Weather	39
Spanish for walkers and motorists	40
Dogs and other nuisances	42
Organisation of the walks	43
THE WALKS	
● 1 Around Lobos	44
● 2 From Corralejo to El Cotillo	49
● 3 The crater route	53
● 4 Fuentes de El Chupadero	57
● 5 Clifftop walk from El Cotillo	58
● 6 Cañada de Melián	62
● 7 From Tindaya to La Oliva	64
● 8 From Tetir to Tefía	66
● 9 From Tefía to Tetir	69
● 10 Puertito de Los Molinos circuit	70
● 11 Embalse de los Molinos	73
● 12 From Antigua to Betancuria	77
● 13 Mirador de Morro Velosa	80
● 14 From Betancuria to Vega de Río Palmas	83
● 15 From Tiscamanita to Vega de Río Palmas	85

4 Landscapes of Fuerteventura

- 16 Barranco de las Peñitas — 88
- 17 From Vega de Río Palmas to Ajuy — 91
- 18 Ajuy's sea caves and Playa del Jurado — 92
- 19 Five-star Ajuy circuit — 94
- 20 Las Salinas and Puerto de la Torre — 98
- 21 Pozo Negro circuit via La Atalayita — 101
- 22 From Giniginamar to Tarajalejo — 102
- 23 Montaña Cardón — 105
- 24 The Pared isthmus — 106
- 25 El Jable — 110
- 26 Pico de la Zarza — 114
- 27 From Barranco Gran Valle to Cofete — 118
- 28 From Morro Jable to Costa Calma along the beach — 122
- 29 The Sotavento lagoon — 126
- 30 The tip of the island — 127

Car tour 4: A DAY OUT ON LANZAROTE — 132
Playa Blanca • El Golfo • Yaiza • Parque Nacional de Timanfaya • Tinajo • La Santa • Monumento al Campesino • La Geria • Uga • Femés • Playa Blanca

WALKS ON LANZAROTE
- 31 Montaña Roja — 140
- 32 The rock pools of Janubio — 144
- 33 Punta de Papagayo — 146
- 34 Atalaya de Femés — 148
- 35 Degollada del Portugués — 149

Bus and ferry timetables — 150
Index — 151
Touring maps — *inside back cover*

The parish church at La Oliva, Nuestra Señora de la Candelaria, overpowers the village with its solid black-stone bell tower (Car tour 3, Walk 7).

Preface

Fuerteventura is different from all the other islands in the Canaries. Being the closest to Africa, there's a definite taste of the Sahara about it. The landscape is thirsty, barren and severe.

In two things this island excels and outdoes all the others in the archipelago: it has the best beaches and the best climate. Beaches are what Fuerteventura is all about — mile upon mile of untouched golden sand, great billowing white sand dunes, foaming surf, and quiet turquoise coves. If you're after sea and sun, this is the island for you! Windsurfers, too, have discovered the perfect winds to enjoy their hobby.

Although the scenery changes little, it's pleasant to tour Fuerteventura's timeless landscapes by car. The island's beauty spots are tucked away, often out of sight. I hope this book will help you find them. But please — if you are hiring a jeep or a bike, keep to the main tracks and do not travel cross-country: Fuerteventura's dunes are home to very rare birds, some of which lay their well-camouflaged eggs directly on the ground. To protect these birds, some parts of the island are under state protection — for instance, the dunes of Corralejo.

In case you get tired of the beaches (which is fairly unlikely), or there's an overcast, cool day, there are some fine walks to be enjoyed on Fuerteventura. You needn't be an inveterate hiker: there are walks to suit all appetites — rambles across the old worn hills, fairly easy mountain ascents, seaside hikes and, for explorers, rocky *barrancos* in which to flounder. Even the picnic spots will help you get better acquainted with the island. There are hidden streams, palm groves, and crystal-clear lagoons just waiting to be discovered. Lobos — the tiny island of 'anthills' — is another world again. It's a charmer.

Fuerteventura is the richest of the islands in Guanche relics (sorry, Gran Canaria). Few people are aware of this. The island is littered with Guanche settlements. (Here on Fuerteventura the aboriginals were called Majos.) Unfortunately, they are mostly unprotected and crumbling away. Admittedly, most are hard to distinguish or are well off the beaten track; hence I've only mentioned a couple of these sites in the book, the major one being La Atalayita (Walk 21).

6 Landscapes of Fuerteventura

Tourism, after having side-stepped this island for many years, struck suddenly like a bolt of lightning, leaving the populace reeling from the blow. Being reserved in character by nature, they were very wary of it all. So at first you may not find all the Fuerteventurans as openly friendly as other Canarians. Speaking some Spanish can make a big difference, especially amongst the village folk and those not involved in tourism.

Landscapes of Fuerteventura will, I hope, give you a better insight into this now-booming tourist mecca.

— NOEL ROCHFORD

Acknowledgements

Thanks to Conny Spelbrink and to my publishers, Sunflower, who between them, rewalked all the routes for the 7th edition and added several new routes. Thanks also to Jan Kostura who guides walkers on all the Canary Islands and who revised the walks in this 8th edition while preparing for his future trips to the island — and contributed many new photos.

Further reading

Titles in the 'Landscapes' series are countryside guides, intended for use in tandem with a general guide — of which there are many available. Two reference books which I particularly treasure are *Wild Flowers of the Canary Islands* by David and Zoë Bramwell and *Crafts and Traditions of the Canary Islands* by Michael Eddy. Both are out of print at time of writing, but available on the web from various suppliers (at hefty prices, so try your local library first!).

If you enjoy using this book, I've written several other 'Landscapes' for the Canaries: *Tenerife (Orotava • Anaga • Teno • Cañadas); Southern Tenerife and La Gomera; La Palma and El Hierro; Lanzarote; Gran Canaria*. To get a taste of *all* the islands, there is also my *walking* guide, *Canary Island Walks* covering nine islands. All are published by Sunflower Books.

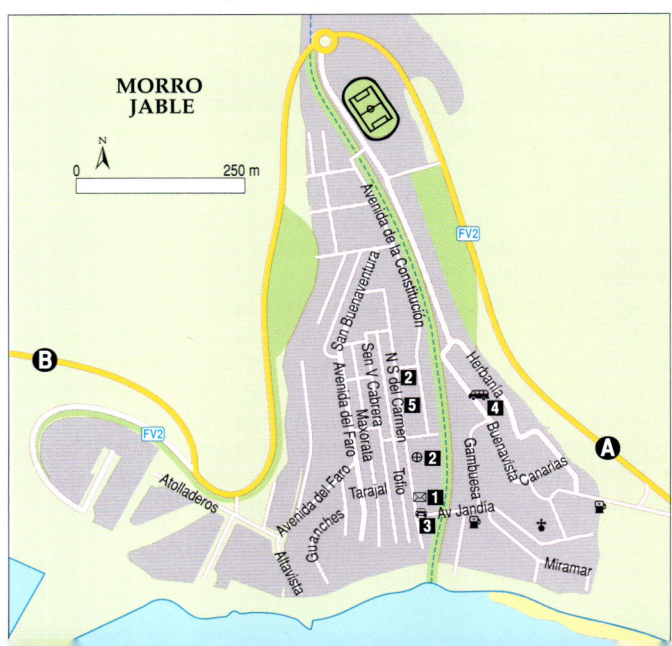

Getting about

On Fuerteventura it's a good idea to hire a vehicle for at least part of your holiday. **Car hire** on the island is very reasonable, with all hire firms offering competitive rates.

Coach tours are easy to arrange and get you to all the tourist points of interest, but never off the beaten track.

There is a very good **local bus** service between the resorts themselves and to/from Puerto del Rosario. But buses to inland villages are still severely limited (often just one a day), so you may need private transport to reach any hikes in these outposts. Selected bus timetables are shown on page 126, but you may find more convenient buses operating from your resort once you are on the island. Don't rely *solely* on our timetables. Re-check the timetables at **www.tiadhe.com**, where you'll also find information about bus fares. Although some buses may run late, I'd advise you *always to arrive 15 minutes early!*

Taxis fares are not particularly high, but you *do* have to travel long distances to get anywhere. Sharing with others lessens the blow. There are no Uber or similar on demand services on the island at present. At all the major resorts you will find a list of prices to the most common destinations — usually at the taxi stand. If you want to know approximately how much your journey will cost, you can compare distances with one of the more popular routes before you set off. Below are the telephone numbers of the major taxi operators. *It's best to book 24 hours in advance to assure a place!*

Airport 902-404704
Antigua 928-878011
Betancuria 928-163004
Puerto Rosario 928-850216
Caleta de Fuste/Castillo
   928-163004; 928-166510
Corralejo 928-537441,
   928-866108
Costa Calma 609-274180
Gran Tarajal 928-870059
La Lajita 928-161110
La Oliva 928-866108
Pájara (Morro Jable taxi)
   928-541257; (Costa
   Calma taxi) 928-547032
Tuineje 928-870059

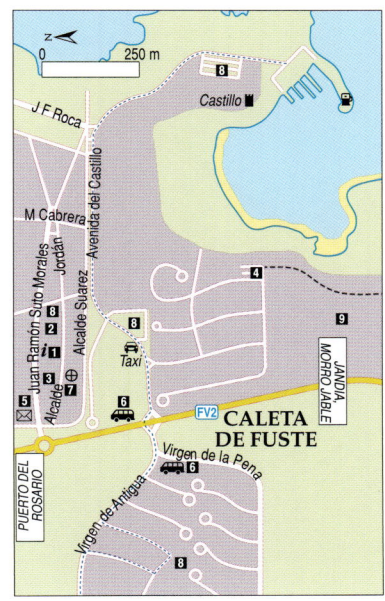

8 Landscapes of Fuerteventura

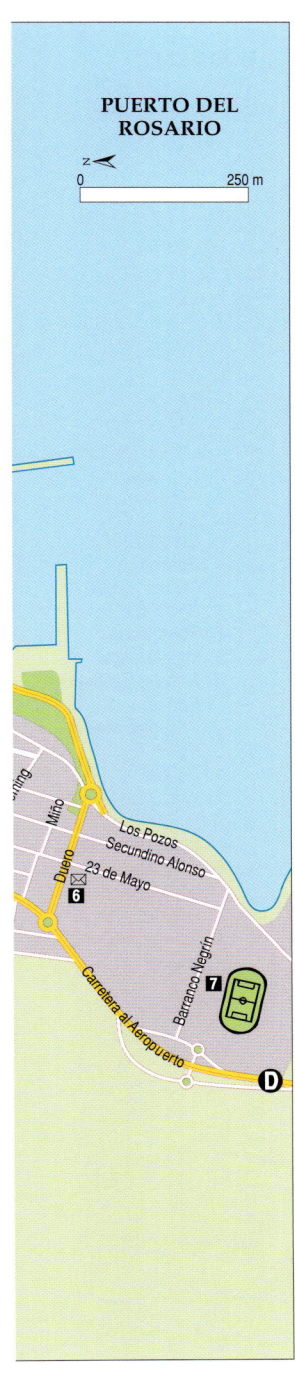

PUERTO DEL ROSARIO
1. Tourist information
2. Bus station
3. Casa Museo de Unamuno
4. Town hall and police
5. Island council (Cabildo)
6. Post office
7. Sports ground
8. (near Exit B) Medio Ambiente offices
9. Medical centre
10. Nuestra Señora del Rosario
- **A** to Corralejo
- **B** to La Oliva
- **C** to Casillas del Angel
- **D** to hospital and airport

GRAN TARAJAL
1. Tourist information
2. Telephones
3. Medical centre
4. Taxi rank
5. Post office
6. Bus stop
7. Police
8. Market
9. San Diego
- **A** to Tuineje

10 Landscapes of Fuerteventura

Picnics and short walks

Most tourists come here for the beaches and the sunshine. There are enough beautiful beaches on this island to visit a different one each day for a month. Many of them are off the beaten track, and this means taking along a picnic if you will spend the day there. And carry a large umbrella because there is generally little or *no* shade (indicated by ○ in our picnic titles).

Finding other picnic spots, however, is a different story. There's no wealth of 'organised' picnic places on Fuerteventura, unlike on some of the other Canary Islands. The picnic settings I've suggested are therefore natural beauty spots I've discovered on my walks. My own personal favourite is Lobos … when it's not too windy!

On the following pages you'll find my suggestions for some lovely picnic spots, together with all the information you need to reach them. *Note that picnic numbers correspond to walk numbers,* so you can quickly find the general location on the island by referring to the pull-out touring map (where the walks are highlighted in green/white). Most of the spots I've chosen are easy to reach, and I include transport details, walking times, and views or setting — as well as page references for maps and photos. The *precise* location of the picnic spot is shown on the relevant large-scale *walking* map by the symbol *P*.

While I've recommended a car for getting to and from almost all these picnic spots, many are accessible by bus as well — you'll just have a somewhat longer walk. (**These picnic suggestions make ideal short walks however you are getting about on the island.**) Please read the country code on page 15 and go quietly in the countryside. *Buen provecho!*

1 LOBOS (map page 48, photos on pages 44-45 and 46-47) ○

Access by 🚢 ferry from Corralejo to/from Lobos: 10-15min on foot. Head left from the jetty; less than 10min along, take a path off left, into the sand dunes — to lovely Playa de La Calera. If you prefer swimming off rocks, try the stunning setting of Casas El Puertito just 5min from the jetty — *to the right*. Both are superb, tranquil spots. ***No shade!***

2 FARO DE EL TOSTON (touring map, photo on pages 50-51) ○

Access by 🚗 to/from the Faro de El Tostón: 5-10min on foot. Park at the side of the road to the lighthouse, north of El Cotillo. Picnic at any of the delightful turquoise coves or on the dunes nearby. ***No shade!***

3 HERDERS SHELTER (map and photos on pages 54-55) ○

Access by 🚗 only: from the FV109 3km east of Lajares follow the

Side-on view to the Casa de los Coroneles at La Oliva (Walk 7). Behind the building is a palm-shaded ruin from where you can look out at the perfectly formed volcanic cone of Montaña del Frontón (Picnic 7)

smooth dirt road across the cycle path to waypoint ❸; park and walk to ❷ (10-15min on foot). Use the map to peer into Calderón Hondo while you're there!

7 LA OLIVA (map on pages 64-65, photos above and on page 35)

Access by 🚌 (Lines: 07, 08): 10-15min on foot. From the bus stop, walk to the Casa de los Coroneles, signposted from the church. Or by 🚗: 5min on foot. Park in the car park in front of the *Casa* in La Oliva. Take the track at the right of the outbuildings to reach a ruined homestead directly behind the Casa de los Coroneles. This is a pleasant spot from where you can admire the setting without the tourists, or look out east to the impressive Montaña del Frontón. Some places to sit in the shade from a few palms or the walls of this derelict, but charming homestead.

9 TEFIA (map and photo on pages 68-69)

Access by 🚌 (Line 02): 10-15min on foot. From the bus stop, follow Walk 9 on page 69 to the pretty Ermita de San Augustín. Or by 🚗: 2min on foot; drive to the *ermita*. Picnic in the shady courtyard, where there is seating. Utterly peaceful.

10 BARRANCO DE LOS MOLINOS (map on page 71, photos on pages 70-71 and 72)

Access by 🚗: 10min on foot. Park in the car park at waypoint ❺, just past Las Parcelas. Walk straight ahead to the hide, where there is a bench in the shade protecting you from the afternoon sun. Picnic while watching the birds and enjoy the 'green curtain' of the *barranco*.

13 CONVENTO DE SAN BUENAVEN-TURA (map and photo on page 82)

Access by 🚗 or 🚌 (Line 02) to/from Betancuria: 10-15min on foot. Follow the Short walk on page 80 and picnic in shade of the convent ruins or in the pretty *barranco* below.

14 BETANCURIA (map on page 82)

Access by 🚗 or 🚌 (Line 02) to/from Betancuria: 15-20min on foot, with a steady climb of up to 100m/330ft. Follow Short walk 14 on page 83 out of Betancuria and picnic anywhere on the grassy slopes above the last houses … out of sight of the dogs, or you'll get no peace! There is a good outlook down to the village. There is no shade until you get up into the stubby pines.

16 BARRANCO DE LAS PEÑITAS (map on pages 90-91, photos on pages 42, 88-89 and opposite) ○

Access by 🚗 or 🚌 (Line 02) to/from the 'Casa de la Naturaleza' bus stop on the Presa de las Peñitas road in Vega de Río Palmas, as described in 'Transport' on page 76: 30-40min on foot. Follow Walk 16

Landscape at the Presa de las Peñitas (near Picnic 16)

on page 88 to reach the dam wall and descend *with care* to the chapel (Nuestra Señora de la Peña), which offers the only shade in this sun-baked setting — but no peace and quiet these days, as so many people follow this trail.

18 CALETA NEGRA (map page 92, photo on page 97, top) ○
Access by 🚗: 15-20min on foot. Park at the turning circle at the entrance to Ajuy, in the village itself, or on the beach. Follow the path on the right-hand side of the beach uphill — in other words, just follow the rest of the crowd. Then use the notes for Walk 18 on page 93 to reach the cliffs not far above the *mirador*, from where you can continue around the bay — not too close to the edge! — in welcome solitude. ***No shade.***

19 BARRANCO DE LA MADRE DEL AGUA (map on page 95, photo on pages 94-95)
Access by 🚗: 7-10min on foot. Park in the *barranco* bed, near Ajuy. To get there, take the Ajuy road out of Pájara (FV621), and after 9km turn off onto a track, just past a lone house (on a bend in the road, just *before* you come into Ajuy). Park in the *barranco* bed or, if you have a four-wheel drive vehicle, you can drive up to the picnic spot. Head up the bed of the *barranco* for 7min, until you reach a narrow valley choked with palms. A little way in, you'll find a lovely little brook with a footbridge. Picnicking in a setting like this is rare indeed on Fuerteventura!

20 PUERTO DE LA TORRE (map on page 99, photo on page 100)
Access by 🚗: 5min on foot. Park at Puerto de la Torre: take the Las Salinas turn-off from the FV2 (3km south of Caleta de Fuste). Drive into Las Salinas, then continue south, first along the road and then along a short stretch of track, to Puerto de la Torre. The best place to picnic is in the thin grove of palms which offers plenty of shade, five minutes back off the beach.

22 GINIGINAMAR (map on pages 102-103) ○
Access by 🚗: 10-15min on foot, with a steep gravelly climb at the start. Park in Giniginamar. Walk to the right-hand (western) end of the beach and climb the gravelly path up the hillside behind the houses for a good view over this quiet little fishing village and along the coastline. ***No shade.***

27 PLAYA DE COFETE (map on page 120, photos on pages 118-119 and the cover) ○
Access by 🚗 *(jeep or 4-wheel drive recommended)*: up to 5min on foot. Take the first left outside Cofete hamlet (Car tour 2) to the beaches of Cofete and Barlovento de Jandía. Park on the beach. Picnic anywhere. Note that the sea is very dangerous; treat it with respect. ***No shade.***

Touring

Most visitors to Fuerteventura hire a vehicle for all or part of their stay. Car hire is not expensive. Do shop around, while at the same time bearing in mind that cheapest is not always best! Always check your vehicle in advance and point out any existing dents, scratches, etc. Ask for all the conditions and insurance cover in writing, in English. Check to make sure you have a sound spare tyre and all the necessary tools. Be sure to get the office *and the after-hours* telephone numbers of the car hire firm and carry them with you. If you're not 100% happy about the car, don't take it. Finally, if you pay by credit card, make a note of exactly what you're signing for. *Important:* Leave nothing of value in your car, and always lock it. Car theft is not unknown.

The touring notes are brief: they contain little history or information readily available in free tourist office leaflets or standard guide books. The main tourist centres and towns are not described either, for the same reason. Instead, I concentrate on the 'logistics' of touring: times and distances, road conditions, and seeing places many tourists miss. Most of all I emphasise possibilities for **walking** and **picnicking**. While some of the references to walks and picnics off the beaten track may not be suitable during a long car tour, you may see a landscape that you would like to explore at leisure another day, when you've more time to stretch your legs.

The large fold-out touring map is designed to be held out opposite the touring notes and contains all the information you will need outside the towns. **Town plans**, showing exits for motorists, are on pages 6-10. The two largest resorts on the island are Corralejo in the north and Morro Jable in the south, so I based the drives around these two centres, but they can easily be joined from other, more central, fast-growing holiday resorts like Caleta de Fuste.

Remember to allow plenty of time for visits, and to take along warm clothing as well as some food and drink, in case you are delayed. The distances in the touring notes are *cumulative* from the departure point. A key to the **symbols** in the touring notes is on the touring map.

All motorists should read the country code opposite and go quietly in the countryside. *Buen viaje!*

A country code for walkers and motorists

The experienced rambler is used to following a country code, but the tourist out for a lark may unwittingly cause damage, harm animals, or even endanger his own life. Please heed this advice.

- **Do not light fires.**
- **Do not frighten animals.**
- The **dunes** in the north as well as in the south are the home of very rare birds, some of which lay their well-camouflaged eggs directly on the ground. They could easily be destroyed by jeeps or mountain bikes, so please *keep to the main tracks and do not travel cross-country*.
- **Walk quietly** through all hamlets and villages.
- **Leave all gates just as you find them.**
- **Protect all wild and cultivated plants.** Don't try to pick wild flowers or uproot saplings. Obviously fruit and other crops are someone's private property and should not be touched. Never walk over cultivated land.
- **Take all your litter away with you.**
- **Walkers —** *Do not take risks!* This is the most important point of all. Do not attempt walks beyond your capacity, and do not wander off the paths described here if there is any sign of mist or if it is late in the day. Never walk alone (four is the best walking group), and always tell a responsible person exactly where you are going and what time you plan to return. Remember, if you become lost or injure yourself, it may be a long time before you are found. On any but a short walk close to villages, be sure to take a compass, whistle, torch, extra water and warm clothing — as well as some high-energy food, like chocolate. Read and re-read the important note on page 2, as well as guidelines on grade and equipment for each walk you plan to do!

On the Cofete track you're likely to encounter wild donkeys demanding a 'toll'!

Car tour 1: THE BEST OF FUERTEVENTURA
Morro Jable • La Pared • Pájara • Betancuria • Antigua • Gran Tarajal • Las Playitas • Morro Jable

190km/118mi; 5 hours' driving; Exit A from Morro Jable
En route: Picnics 13, 14, 16, 18, 19, 22 (see pages 11-13 and P symbol in the text); Walks 12-19, 22-26, 28, 29; Walk 11 is accessible by detour
The main north-south road (FV2) is generally good — in places motorway standard. Inland roads are good, but narrow. Between Pájara and Vega de Río Palmas the road is quite high and winding. It can be very windy.

Opening hours
Iglesia Santa María and adjacent Museo de Arte Sacro (Betancuria): 09.30-17.00 Mon-Fri, 09.30-14.00 Sat;
Casa Museo (of archaeology; Betancuria) 10.00-17.00 Tue-Sat, 11.00-14.00 Sun;
Windmill Crafts Centre (Antigua) 10.00-18.00 daily;
Windmill Interpretation Centre (Tiscamanita) 10.00-18.00 daily;
Aloe Vera Exclusive (Tiscamanita): 10.00-17.30 Mon-Fri, 10-14 Sat

This drive takes you to some of the best sights on the island, from the most stunning beaches to the most picturesque valleys. You will be treated not only to the beauty spots, but also to the geographical and geological wonders of the island. And the final ingredient to flavour this tour to perfection is the little village of Betancuria — Fuerteventura's ancient former capital.

Leaving Morro Jable, take the FV2 (Exit A). Out of the eyesore of development that is quickly spreading north, you wind in and out of the deep bare *barrancos* that cleave the mountainous backbone of the Jandía Peninsula. Pick up the FV2 expressway at Club Aldiana (where Walk 28 starts). Pico de la Zarza (806m/2645ft), the island's highest summit, can be seen at the end of both the Vinamar and Butihondo valleys. It's a modest peak that rises a mere shoulder above its off-siders. On a fine day, however, you can have a most enjoyable hike there (Walk 26). Leave the expressway at the sign 'Butihondo' and follow the old road (FV602) north towards 'El Salmo'.

Just as you leave the Barranco los Canarios (16km ✖🅿), you go under the expressway, round a bend and come the **Mirador del Salmo** with a stunning view over (📷) captivating **Playa de Sotavento de Jandía★** — the queen of Fuerteventura's beaches. A track forks right off the viewpoint on the bend in the road here and descends to the beach. You could drive down this track — or down the road signposted to 'Playa de Sotavento' 3km further on: this road leads to the glorious part of the beach shown on pages 124-125 — a lagoon framed by an expansive sand bar, where the sea is dotted with a myriad of colourful windsurfs and kites. Sotavento is the highlight of marathon Walk 28 and easy Walk 29; the latter begins at the Hotel Meliá Fuerteventura another 2.5km north. To the north are the giant sand hills of the Pared isthmus. Just before you reach Costa Calma, wind generators come into view through the hills on the left (photo on page 108).

16

Car tour 1: The best of Fuerteventura

They're landmarks on Walks 24 and 25, both of which start at Costa Calma and cross the isthmus. **Costa Calma** (25km ⛰️🏠✕🚌) has tried to mitigate the worst effects of touristic development with beautiful landscaping.

Some 27km from Morro Jable, at a roundabout 1.5km beyond Costa Calma, turn off left for La Pared (FV605). **La Pared** (32km ⛰️✕⚓), is a pretty *urbanización* with lots of greenery — an oasis in the desolate and naked landscape on the outskirts of the dunes. Continuing towards Pájara, cloud-catching hills rise on the right — Montaña Cardón (691m/2265ft), setting for Walk 23, is the highest. The landscape is a mixture of sharp ridges and smooth rounded hills. You pass the quiet cultivated valley of **Huertas de Chilegua** (✕), and the road climbs into these smooth rounded hills — ochre-coloured mounds of the the oldest hill formations on the island. Crossing a pass at the **Mirador de Sicasumbre** (📷), without even getting out of the car you have an unsurpassed view of the sea on the left and inland down a narrow valley — the actual viewpoints are up hills left and right. A sea of ridges and valleys cuts up the bleak landscape ahead. Soon after, a *'zona militar'* sign warns that you're passing a prohibited area (a firing range).

Right: the wrecked freighter mentioned on the next page. Below: the Barranco de las Peñitas, one of the island's most picturesque valleys, is visited later in the tour.

18 Landscapes of Fuerteventura

Descending to another isolated farmstead, watch for small earthen reservoirs in the valley floor. These are called *presas secas* (dry reservoirs), because they have been built to catch the water that comes down the *barrancos,* but they do not retain it. The water passes through the permeable soil into wells which have been sunk some 17-20m (about 60ft) below the ground in front of these *presas.* The small metal windpumps (like the one in the photo on page 17) are used to bring this water up to ground level again.

Through the hills, down on the coast, you may catch sight of a shipwreck washed ashore. If you want to see it at close quarters, allow for a detour of some 15km and take the gravel road forking off sharp left some 8.5km down from the pass, with a sign, 'Lugar La Solapa'. Go down all the way to the coast and, just before reaching the beach (Playa La Solapa), turn left for about 3.5km to Playa Garcey and the shipwreck.

Closer to Pájara the hills open out into a vast depression. Meet a junction (54km) and turn sharp left on the FV621, to descend to Ajuy. Rounding a bend, you look down into a valley lush with palm trees, tamarisk shrubs and garden

Car tour 1: The best of Fuerteventura

plots. Watch for the small ravine crammed with palms cutting back off it, into the hills running down on the right. This ravine, the Barranco de la Madre del Água (*P*19), boasts the only permanently flowing stream on Fuerteventura. It's only a trickle, but the picnic spot is enchanting (photo on pages 94-95).

Ajuy (63km; Walks 17-19), the small village set on the edge of a black-sand beach shown on page 92, is one of two fishing settlements on the west coast. The dramatically sited ancient port here is well worth a visit, as is the Mirador Caleta Negra (📷).

This viewpoint (photo on page 97), and the port itself, lie north of the village, some 10 minutes' walk around the cliffs — just follow the crowds! The *mirador* sits in the cliff-face like a balcony, from where you look straight across to some sea caves. You can also take steps down into two sea caves directly below the viewpoint. Read about them in the photo caption on page 96! But after visiting the *mirador*, I'd suggest you follow the notes for Walk 18 to get away from the crowds (*P*18) since, fortunately, few tourists venture beyond the viewpoint. Just keep well away from the edge of the cliffs!

From Ajuy return to the junction and keep straight on to **Pájara** (74km 🍴🏔✕. This is a large farming community surrounded by hills. The shady village is a welcoming sight, with its abundance of trees and small colourful gardens. Don't miss the church here; it is especially noteworthy for the striking 'Aztec' stone-carved decoration above the main entrance. Quite a curiosity because, along with a similar lot of sculptures in La Oliva, these carvings are unique in the Canary Islands. The two naves inside the church date back to 1645 and 1687, while the carving over the door is thought to date from the 1500s.

Leaving Pájara, take the road signposted for 'Betancuria' (FV30); it's at the left of the church. Again you ascend into the hills, climbing a sometimes narrow, winding road that hugs the sheer inclines (some people

The church at Pájara, dedicated to the Virgen de la Regla, is especially noted for the much-photographed 'Aztec' stone carvings around the main entrance.

might find this stretch unnerving, although it is built up at the side). There are excellent views back over the Barranco de Pájara. The (unsigned) **Degollada de los Granadillos** with the **Mirador del Risco de Las Peñas** on the left (📷) is the pass that takes you over a solid spur of rock jutting out into the valley below. From here you have a superb outlook over to the enclosing rocky ridges.

Soon, descending, you come to another parking area, the **Mirador de las Peñitas** (📷), overlooking the **Presa de las Peñitas**, a reservoir lodged in the V of the Barranco de las Peñitas, shown on page 91. It looks deeper than it is, since it has filled up with silt; lately it's completely dry all year round. Groves of tamarisk trees huddle around the tail of the *presa*, and that's a good spot from which to do some bird-watching. Green gardens step the sides of the slopes, and palm trees complement the scene. Below the reservoir lies a sheer-sided rocky ravine, the ideal hiding place for the chapel dedicated to the island's patron saint, Nuestra Señora de la Peña (🅿16; photo on pages 88-89). This impressive ravine is one of the island's particular beauty spots.

Soon the rest of the valley opens up, with houses set amidst a healthy sprinkling of palms and cultivated plots. The first turning below the *mirador* is a sharp left, signposted 'Vega de Río Palmas' (85km): it leads after a little over 1km to the tapas café (🍴), shown on page 24 and the starting point

Car tour 1: The best of Fuerteventura

for Walks 16 and 17. (This detour is *not* included in the main touring distances.) Keep ahead and come the church in **Vega de Río Palmas** (85km ♣✕), on the right and also dedicated to Nuestra Señora de la Peña. Walks 14 and 15 end here ... perhaps with a visit to the excellent bar/restaurant Don Antonio beside the church.

At the end of this valley you come to the village of **Betancuria★** (90km ♣♠✕M; photo on page 77), well hidden from the marauding Berbers of earlier centuries. It's a very picturesque collection of manorial buildings, with a grand 17th-century cathedral dedicated to Santa María. The cathedral and convent here are the oldest examples of their style in the archipelago. Relics abound in historic Betancuria. A number of the old houses have doorways and arches dating back to the 15th century. Betancuria was the capital of Fuerteventura for some 400 years, up until 1835, and was also the first episcopal seat for all the Canaries. The oldest part of the village huddles around the cathedral, where many of the once-neglected buildings have been restored. History-hunters will enjoy the cathedral and the small Museo de Arte Sacro — as well as the nearby Casa Museo on the main road. Walk 12 ends in Betancuria, having followed an old pilgrims' route over the hills from Antigua. Walk 13, to the viewpoint shown on pages 80-81, begins and ends here; Walk 14 starts here and heads over the hills (*P*14) to Vega de Río Palmas via the island's only 'pine forest'.

Continuing north on the FV30 out of Betancuria, everyone passes by the beautiful 15th-century Franciscan convent of **San Buenaventura** (*P*13), the shell of which sits below the road on the right. Inside it (unseen from the road) are the beautiful cloistered arches shown on page 82. There is also a small enclosed church near the convent — the first church on the island (but much rebuilt in the 17th century). As you zigzag up out of the valley, you can either pull over at the top of the pass at the **Mirador Guize y Ayose** with its two 4m/12ft-high bronze statues of aboriginal (Majo) kings — my suggestion — or turn up right to the **Mirador de Morro Velosa** on a hilltop above the pass (☞✕M). This *mirador*, the goal of

The church in Vega de Río Palmas, with the lovely restaurant Don Antonio at the right of the square

The seaside nucleus of Las Playitas is still unspoilt.

Walk 13 referred to above, is closed at present for rebuilding, and it is not known when it will reopen. It can be dreadfully crowded: if you drive to it (when it reopens), make sure your car won't be trapped by tour coaches! From either vantage point there is a fine panorama over a vast plain to the north. Its far-distant reaches are edged by sharp abrupt hills called *cuchillos* (knives); over to the left lie *morros* (low, smooth hills). Betancuria nestles cosily in the valley floor below. Those of you familiar with the work of Lanzarote's César Manrique will find the Morro Velosa *mirador* building itself of interest, as Manrique supervised its planning. Inside, there will be an exhibition about Fuerteventura's protected areas and species.

Descending, you soon pass the turn-off left to Valle de Santa Inés and Llanos de la Concepción (Walk 11), while you continue ahead on the FV416 for Antigua. Another expansive plain stretches out below you now, edged by the buildings of Antigua. Entering **Antigua** (100km ✝︎▲✕☕), you come to the beautifully laid-out square shown on ages 78-79, with its simple but nevertheless imposing 18th-century church. Walk 12 starts here. Just north of Antigua (on the Puerto del

Car tour 1: The best of Fuerteventura

Rosario road) stands **El Molino★**, a well-preserved 200-year-old windmill, once used for grinding corn. This is part of the Antigua Windmill Crafts Centre (✕MWC). The windmill *(molino)* is an appropriate introduction to Antigua, because this area has the highest concentration of windmills on Fuerteventura. Next door is the Majorero (Goat) Cheese Museum.

Now following the FV20 south towards Tuineje, you're out in the country again. Palms return to the scene, and a trickle of villages is seen sitting back in the plain. Threading your way through hills, you find cultivated fields sheltering along the floors of the *barrancos*. You clip the edge of **Valles de Ortega**, but **Água de Bueyes** (106km ✕) is the next village en route. Its less common windmill, the *molina*, is shown on page 36. Three dark volcanoes — La Laguna, Liria and Los Arrabales — rupture the lake of lava that spills out over the plains on the left. This area is called the *malpais* ('badlands'), and the eruptions from these volcanoes created the AA-lava landscape visited in Walk 21. A restored windmill sits at the entrance to **Tiscamanita** (109km ✕); here you'll find the Windmill Interpretation Centre. On the outskirts of the village, you may like to call at the Aloe Vera Exclusive factory, for a stimulating introduction to the benefits of the plant. Around **Tuineje** (112km ☏) the large *fincas* of the tomato-growers are a prominent feature in a barren landscape.

You now keep on the FV20, passing through an industrial area, to your next port of call — **Gran Tarajal** (125km ▲☏✕⊕). Coming into one of the island's biggest towns, you look out over lean groves of palms dispersed along the valley floor. Tamarisk *(tarajal)* shrubs add to the verdure. This once-important port has a small commercial centre and attractive boulevard lining the beach. The houses step back up the steep sides of the *barranco* and overlook the black-sand beach that curves around it.

Leaving Gran Tarajal, turn off right on the FV512, eventually passing an eyesore of development. Under 1km further on you come to the burgeoning development spreading out from the nucleus of the island's prettiest seaside village, **Las Playitas** (131km ▲✕). Built on sheer rocky outcrops which rise out of the mouth of the *barranco*, it conceals a lovely dark-sand beach stretching out behind it.

Detour: Curiosity-seekers may like to drive from Las Playitas to El Faro de Entallada, the fortress-like lighthouse shown overleaf. It's set at the mouth of a wide bare valley, some 6km further north. A tarred road (very narrow for the last kilometre) on the right leads out to it, on your return from Las Playitas. Just below the lighthouse is a spectacular *mirador* with views all the away to Jandía.

Homeward bound, from Las Playitas return to the FV4 and keep right. Then go left on the FV2 for 'Morro Jable'. Winding behind great coastal valleys, some 6.5km from the Gran Tarajal junction you pass the turn-off for the small fishing village of Giniginamar (▲✕*P*22). If you'd like to visit it, the detour will take 8km return. Giniginamar is the starting point for Walk 22 — a very scenic, but somewhat vertigious, coastal hike to Tarajalejo.

Tarajalejo (152km ▲▲▲✕ and ☏4km to the north) lies either

Above: the Casa de la Naturaleza in Vega de Río Palmas is a super place to take a break, full of greenery and with a mini 'lake' inside. Left: the well-kept plants of Aloe Vera Exclusive and the Faro de Entallada

side of the FV2. The resort, to the left, occupies the end of a sweeping beach. Short walk 22 starts and ends here. Some 4km further on, you pass a turn-off left for the small tourist resort of La Lajita (⬧✕). Just past this turn-off is the beautifully landscaped **Oasis Park★** — a zoo, garden centre, and camel station offering rides. The camel trains crossing the hills on the left here as you leave the valley really do make an impressive sight.

Now climb amidst low hills, snatching views of pretty coves with not a soul about. Mounting the top of a crest, you join the expressway with fine views of Jandía, encompassing the mountainous backbone and identical twin peaks of Zarza (Walk 26) and Mocán, and the luminous blue and green ribbon of beaches that are the fame of Fuerteventura. Soon you're back in **Morro Jable** (190km).

Car tour 2: PUNTA DE JANDIA AND THE WEST COAST
Morro Jable • Punta de Jandía • Cofete • Morro Jable

71km/44mi; 3-4 hours driving; Exit B from Morro Jable
En route: Picnic 27 (see page 13 and **P** symbol in the text); Walks 27, 30

Except for a 10km stretch of narrow tarred road at the tip of the island, the rest of the drive is on a rough gravel road — the worst part being the leg to Cofete. In the winter this drive is only recommended for 4WD vehicles, especially the Cofete stretch (which is also very narrow and may be unnerving for some motorists and passengers). If you decide to venture off in a standard hired car, read what your rental agreement says about travelling on unsurfaced roads — and remember that there are no petrol stations out here, and nobody to help if you have car problems. The route is well frequented by jeep safaris, so be alert for the local 'rally drivers' as well as inconsiderate tourists. Avoid this route after wet weather, and note also that the peninsula is usually very windy. Watch out for the wild donkeys that roam these plains — some stop cars in the middle of the track to beg for food quite aggressively!

Opening hours
Villa Winter (for guided tour): daily, 10.00-14.00 and 15.00-17.00

As bleak and unfriendly as this landscape may appear, it is far from unappealing. The wall of ancient volcanic mountains that dominates the Jandía Peninsula harbours severe but striking valleys. An air of loneliness and calm lingers over the plains. Crossing the *cumbre* from east to west you have spectacular views: the mountains become more impressive as they sweep back up into sheer cliffs, the vast beaches more alluring with their pounding surf. The east coast shelters a number of secluded coves, the west coast flourishes splendid sweeps of sand. It's not the kind of place you'd visit to spend a day on the beach: the strong winds will blow sand in your sarnies, not to mention the bumpy ride out. But what makes this tour so alluring are these very discomforts — and the isolation of the area.

Leave Morro Jable via Exit B and turn off right just above the port on a road signposted to 'Cofete'. After 1.5km (past the cemetery) this road reverts to gravel. Heading out into one of the most desolate corners of the island, you bump your way in and out of small deep *barrancos*. Nearly all of them end at pretty sandy coves, usually accessible on rough tracks. Crossing a vast open plain, after 3km you come to a large parking area on the right, with a bus stop and an information board in the setting shown on page 121 (bottom right). From here a stone-edged path heads up into a wide valley (**Gran Valle**) that carves a great gap out of the Jandía massif. This valley offers an alternative route to Cofete — on foot! It's an old mule track that was once the main east/west link; Walk 27 follows it. Note: only about 100 metres up the Gran Valle trail lies a magnificent community of rare *Euphorbia handiensis* (Jandía thistle; see the photo on page 129).

Sharp rocky ridges dominate

The Villa Winter is the main feature of this plain. Read about its fascinating history in Walk 27 (pages 120, 121) and its connection with the Ajuy sea caves (Walk 18, photo caption on page 96).

the landscape. Low salt-resistant vegetation — *cosco, aulaga,* ice plants and *Lycium intricatum* are the inhabitants of this intractable terrain. Goats roam deep in the *barrancos,* and you pass the abandoned tomato plantation of **Casas de Jorós**. Towards the end of the island the plain broadens, and the *barrancos* become less significant. The mountain chain breaks up and slowly subsides into disjointed hills. At Punta de Jandía, the tip of this boot-shaped peninsula, stands the lighthouse.

Some 11.5km out of Morro Jable, you come to the turn-off right for Cofete. Keep left here, to descend to the lighthouse. Tracks branch off to coves ensconced in the low rocky shoreline running along on the left. Approaching Puertito de la Cruz, you come onto a tarred road, which continues on to the lighthouse (*faro*) 1km further on. A lone towering wind generator dwarfs **Puertito de la Cruz** (21km ✕), the village shown on pages 128-129, where Walk 30 begins and ends. The place seems more like a weekend retreat than a fishing hamlet — in summer a lot of caravans take up residence here as well. The small adjoining houses of the old village sit on the edge of the plain, looking out to sea.

Punta de Jandía (☏) itself is unimpressive; however, you do

have a fine view back along the deeply-dissected mountains of the peninsula. Off the point lies an underwater reef called Baja del

The viewpoint at the pass on the descent to Cofete. If you get out of the car, take care: it is so windy that you risk the car door being ripped from its hinges. The view is straight along the golden beaches of Cofete and Barlovento de Jandía.

Griego ('where the Greek sank') or 'Arrecife del Griego' ('Greek's Reef'). Some 200 years ago, a Greek ship carrying passengers from Fuerteventura to Gran Canaria hit it and sank, with all lives lost. A lighthouse on such a long and flat beach is extremely

28 Landscapes of Fuerteventura

Goats, goats, every where ... and sheep getting tangled in spiny aulaga

scenic and has an unusual effect. Next to it is a bar (photo on page 128). Another plus point: swimming from the beach next to the lighthouse is possible and most enjoyable.

Now heading over to the western tip of the peninsula, to Punta Pesebre, return to Puertito de la Cruz and take the sandy track forking left opposite the village. Please heed the sign that warns motorists not to leave the road — this is a protected area. Soon you're overlooking the striking cove shown on page 129, **Playa de Ojos**, bordered by a limpid green sea. Notice the volcanic hues emanating from the cliff walls. **Punta Pesebre** (27km 📷) is much more dramatic than Punta de Jandía on the east coast. You have a spectacular view along the west coast — and to Las Talabijas, the deep maroon volcano on your immediate right. And if the seas are calm, the crystal clear rock pools are brilliant for a cooling dip.

Return along your outgoing route back to the Cofete junction and turn left. *Nervous motorists and passengers be warned:* there is no protective barrier on the track as you zigzag up over a pass to a viewpoint on the left (📷 with limited parking). Take care: it is usually so windy that you risk the car door being ripped off! Here a magnificent vista greets you on the far side of the *cumbre* — one of the best views on the island. You look straight along the golden beaches of Cofete and Barlovento de Jandía. Together they stretch nearly the length of the peninsula. The white-crested breakers and blue-green sea light up the sombre plain and shadowy summits. In the distance rise the billowing sand dunes of the Pared isthmus.

The road, narrow and rough — unnerving for some — is carved out of the steep face of the escarpment. It was built to enable a certain Señor Winter to build his mansion out here. Further down the track, you'll spot a thriving colony of *candelabra,* the large multi-armed, cactus-like plant resembling a chandelier shown on page 121. The villagers once used the latex of this plant to catch fish: they put it into rock pools to stun the fish and bring them to the surface.

Cofete (47km ✖) is a rustic outpost of stone and cement huts and a restaurant with very tasty home cooking. Señor Winter, the German who owned the peninsula, forbade anyone to live here, so it

Car tour 2: Punta de Jandía and the west coast

never grew into a real village. His villa, shown on pages 26-27, is the main feature of the plain.

Pass through Cofete and bear right. After some 200 metres a track forking left leads to a never-ending beach (*P*27). **Important:** the sea here is dangerous at all times. A cross-current runs just off the shore, and a number of tourists have drowned. *Please do not swim!* The Winter residence (now owned by a Gran Canaria hotel chain but occupied by the grandson of a man who laboured on the house, as an unofficial 'museum') is 1.7km away, should your curiosity get the better of you. Read more about it in Walk 27 on pages 120 and 121.

Follow the same route back to **Morro Jable** (71km).

Morro Jable and its lighthouse

Car tour 3: NORTHERN LANDSCAPES
Corralejo • Puerto del Rosario • Tetir • Tefía • Los Molinos • Tindaya • Vallebrón • La Oliva • El Cotillo • Corralejo

130km/81mi; under 5 hours driving; Exit B from Corralejo
En route: Picnics 2, 3, 7, 9, 10 (see pages 12-13 and *P* symbol in the text); Walks 2-10 (Walks 20 and 21 and Picnic 20 are on the alternative route in the footnote below.)
Roads are generally good. Note that it can be very windy along the coast.

Opening hours
La Alcogida Ecomuseum: Tue-Sat from 10.00-17.00 (entrance fee);
Casa de Los Coroneles: Tue-Sat from 10.00-18.00 (entrance fee);
Cueva del Llano: daily from 10.00-18.00 (entrance fee);
Torre de El Tostón (closed for restoration at press date): Tue-Sat from 10.00-17.00 (entrance fee)

The circuit that this tour follows is fascinating rather than 'beautiful'. Impressive hills and volcanoes border the great interior basins of emptiness. During the second half of the tour you wind in and out of a rough sea of lava called the *malpais* — the 'badlands' — a curious sight, with its surprising amount of plant life and greenery. And after the glorious sand dunes of Corralejo, El Cotillo also proves quite a treat, with its cliff-backed beach and dazzling turquoise coves.

Leave Corralejo on the coastal road to Puerto del Rosario (FV104), easily accessed along the narrow one-way Avenida de Grandes Playas (Exit B; plan page 10). Head out through the dunes shown overleaf, a stunning stretch of white shimmering sand further enhanced by the aquamarine sea and the purply-blue hills that rise up in the background. Lobos (Walk 1) stands out clearly on the left, offshore, with its hundreds of little hillocks and guardian volcano. Although these exquisite dunes are a natural park and bird sanctuary, a couple of hotels interrupt this unique stretch of beauty (4.5km ⛰✕).

Out of this mini-desert, you cross a featureless stone-littered plain and pass a failed development on the left now used by 'alternative life-stylers' as an equally failed ashram and then, on the right, a large urbanization called Parque Holandés. The tour really begins beyond **Puerto del Rosario** (30km ⛰▲✕✝🅿⊕M), as you head back northwest via the inland route.* (You *could* bypass the town altogether on the FV3 ring road, picking up the FV10 for Tetir at the first roundabout.)

If you do go into Puerto del Rosario (which has some nice shops and bars), leave town on León y Castillo (on the right-hand

---

*An alternative route back to Corralejo lies further south, via the FV50, then FV20. This would take you to Caleta de Fuste (⛰▲✕*P*20; Walk 20), Antigua (Walk 12) and Casillas del Angel (Walk 14). It's a particularly good route if you're going to Jandía: you'll see the enormous U-shaped valleys beyond Caleta de Fuste. And you could combine a 17km (return) detour to Pozo Negro (▲✕), an out-of-the-way fishing village sprinkled across a lava tongue; some 3km down the FV420 to Pozo Negro is the turn-off for La Atalayita★ (𝕋), an aboriginal village that is the focal point for Walk 21 from Pozo Negro.

Car tour 3: Northern landscapes

One of seven buildings at the ecomuseum La Alcogida in Tefía, a restoration of a traditional rural village of the 19th century. The buildings are all of different sizes and building materials, according to the economic circumstances of the people who lived in them. Some rooms have been converted to workshops, where you can see artisans creating woven goods, pottery, embroidery, and the like. There's a good video of what is on offer at www.museosfuerteventura.com; definitely a visit not to be missed!

side of the church), then Juan de Bethencourt (Exit B; plan on pages 8-9). This leads to the FV10 to La Oliva. A gentle ascent across a stony plain brings you up to the old airport, Los Estancos, and you drive straight through it. Entering a grand U-shaped valley, you pass through **Tetir** (38km; Walks 8 and 9), a well-spread farming village. The enclosing hills are eroded and rocky, bare of vegetation. Montaña Aceitunal (686m/2250ft) dominates the valley with its sharply pointed features. Climbing out of this valley, you reach a higher one and come into the pretty village of **La Matilla** (43km ✕). Another prominent mountain of equal proportions overshadows the village: Montaña Muda (689m/2260ft) — rising above the springs of Walk 4.

Descending from this basin, meet a junction at 45km and head left for 'Tefía' on the FV207. The sprawling farming community of **Tefía** (51km **M**; Walks 8 and 9) sits on the edge of a vast plain. Behind it rises an amphitheatre of hills. Just beyond the well-kept ecomuseum **La Alcogida★** (definitely worth a visit), turn down the first road forking right, the FV221 signposted for 'Las Parcelas/Los Molinos'. Just over 1km along, a restored windmill rises on the right. It was used to grind *gofio,* an important food source on the island. The restoration of all these windmills was financed by the EU.

Wine-coloured *cosco* patches the arid flat. You pass through the pretty, white houses of **Las Parcelas**, a farming settlement

There's a kite festival each year in November on the Corralejo dunes.

built after the construction of the nearby (but out of sight) Embalse de los Molinos — a reservoir visited on Walk 11 from Llanos de la Concepción. Just 1km past the village football ground, as you dip down into the narrow and deep **Barranco de los Molinos**, pull over on the right to a parking area and walk for a few minutes to a viewpoint over the *barranco*. Bird-watchers will want to continue for another couple of minutes to a hide with a bench, shaded in the afternoons (*P*10). At the bottom of the road you come into **Los Molinos** (62km ✕), the tiny fishing hamlet shown on page 72. It huddles off a lovely bay encircled by the rock cliffs at the mouth of the *barranco*. If you're going to eat here, *mariscos* (mixed shellfish) is the dish to order. A permanent flowing stream that empties out into the sea here, and a pond full of ducks, make this a particularly picturesque base for Walk 10.

Return to the junction below La Matilla and head left for 'Tindaya' and 'La Oliva' on the FV10. Rounding a bend, you look over onto the dark sandy volcano of Montaña Quemada. This particular volcano is rather special because at its base there is a modest monument dedicated to the famous Spanish poet Unamuno, who lived in exile on Fuerteventura.

You next pass above **Tindaya** (81km ✕). It spreads across a flattened crest amidst a profusion of faded brown stone walls. Behind the village the great rocky salient of Montaña Tindaya dominates the surrounding countryside with its boldness. The aboriginals (on Fuerteventura called Majos rather than Guanches) regarded it as their holy mountain, where they slaughtered young goats as sacrifices to their gods. A number of important relics from their epoch have been found on the mountain. To protect these, particularly the rock engravings near the summit, it is no longer possible to climb Tindaya.

Just past Tindaya turn right, to ascend to the village of Vallebrón. The road (FV103) winds up and over a pass, before dipping down into the valley. Just at the pass a track veers off sharply right. If you follow it a few hundred metres uphill, you can park and enjoy an expansive view of Tindaya and the surrounding countryside. Rounding a bend in the *barranco,* you look straight up to **Vallebrón** (86km), a cluster of houses cosily set in a hollow amidst thick clumps of prickly pear and stone walls. Short walk 7, a good leg-stretcher, starts and ends here.

From Vallebrón follow the FV103, then the FV102 to the country village of **La Oliva**★ (93km ✝♠✕⚑M). Keep straight along to a T-junction, where a left turn leads to the Casa de los Coroneles and a right turn to the church. The village rests on the edge of a lava flow. Montaña Arena, a mountain of sand, rises up out of the lava in the background. La Oliva was a town of some importance in the 17th century, when the island's military post was stationed here. The official residence was the colonels' house, the **Casa de los Coroneles** (*P*7; photo on page 12). The building was refurbished at the start of the 21st century (and reopened in 2006 by the king and queen of Spain) but is closed as we go to press for another refurbishment. But the various cultural programmes sponsored by its management are still held in La Oliva pending the *Casa* opening again. To the left of the building stand the dilapidated servants' quarters and stables.

One can't help but notice the perfectly shaped Montaña del Frontón rising up in the background of this naked setting; in fact, it's not the isolated cone it appears to be in the photo on page 12, but only the tail of a long ridge. The parish church at La Oliva, Nuestra Señora de la Candelaria, overpowers the village with its solid black-stone belfry (photo on page 4); this is where Walk 7 ends, having climbed from Tindaya via the *mirador* shown on page 40. The Casa del Capellán (chaplain's house), another old building, sits off the side of the Corralejo road, on the left. This house, and a small house in the village, which has a stone façade with an Aztec motif, are other examples of the as yet unexplained Mexican influence seen on Car tour 1 at Pájara church.

From La Oliva you *could* take an alternative route back to base, via Caldereta — a quiet little village with some excellent examples of traditional architecture, from simple farm dwellings to comfortable villas. To get there, return the way you entered La Oliva but, at the turn-off for Vallebrón, keep straight ahead on the FV102.

The main tour, however, now

View through American aloes to Montaña Arena, from the Casa de los Coroneles

Car tour 3: Northern landscapes

makes for El Cotillo. From La Oliva's church, cross the Corralejo road and follow a narrow village road, soon joining the FV10 for El Cotillo. The FV10 road runs alongside pale green lichen-smeared *malpaís;* the fields are fenced off with neat and trim stone walls. Montaña Arena, on your right, makes a noticeable landmark. Follow the lava flow all the way to **El Cotillo** (110km ⬛✕; Walks 2, 5 and 6). This once-quiet little port (photo on page 63), revitalised by tourism, is a tangle of old and new. There are some good seafood restaurants here (and a few rip-offs). The superb beach set below cliffs, shown on pages 52 and 48-61, lies over to the left of the village — off the track leading out past the 17th-century watchtower (Torre de El Tostón, a small exhibition centre currently being restored; ■). If you take an 8km return detour out to the lighthouse, you will find exquisite little coves ensconced in the dark lava coastline (**P**2; photo on pages 50-51).

On your way back to Corralejo, after just over 7km you pass the start of Walk 6 on your right, then come to a roundabout 1km further on. Take the FV109 here, to the very traditional village of **Lajares** (118km ✕). Walk 3 (one of my favourite hikes on the island) starts here. This charming rural settlement lies amidst a maze of dark lava-stone walls. To see the two windmills for which the village is renowned, take the road

Approaching the windmills at Lajares (top): on the left is a molino *(the one shown bottom left is at Valles de Ortega); on the right is a* molina *(at Água de Bueyes)*

forking off right from the next roundabout. A couple of minutes along, this road passes between the two roadside mills. The slender construction on the right is called a *molina:* a wooden contraption that rotates and is built onto the roof of a house. The house normally has a room on either side of the mill. More robust is the *molino:* it's conical and is moved by pushing the long arms, thus rotating the cap with the windmill blades. This building is not inhabited. Both mills were used for grinding *gofio*. The two photos above, although not taken at Lajares, will help you identify them.

Some 3km from Lajares, the FV109 takes you past a dirt road where you could head north for a closer look at the volcano shown on page 54, Calderón Hondo (*P*3), and then to the FV101, where you go left. Or first turn *right* for approximately 1.5km, then follow signs to the Cueva del Llano (∩M), a volcanic tube near Villaverde. There is a small museum and an excellent guided tour of the cave. On your left the dramatic volcanic scenery of Walk 3 unravels its humps and hollows, and the bold red-tinted sentinel of Montaña Bayuyo heralds the end of the tour at **Corralejo** (130km).

Walking

Fuerteventura is a large island, but it does not present a great variety of landscapes to the casual visitor. So I hope you will be pleasantly surprised by the many picturesque corners found on these walks which cover a good cross-section of the island. *There are walks for everyone*.

Beginners: Start on the walks graded ●, and check any short walks — *and the picnics!*

Experienced walkers: If you are accustomed to rough terrain, you should be able to enjoy all these walks. Do take into account the season and weather conditions: don't attempt the more strenuous walks in high summer; protect yourself from the sun and carry ample water.

All walkers: Before you set off, be sure to check for any users' updates on Sunflower's website! See the 'UPDATE' tab on the Fuerteventura page.

Grading, waymarking, maps, GPS

We've tried to give you a quick overview of each walk's **grade** in the Contents. But for full details see the walk itself. Here is a brief overview of the three gradings:

● easy-moderate — ascents/descents of no more than about 300-500m/ 1000-1800ft; good surfaces underfoot; easily followed

● moderate-strenuous — ascents/descents may be over 500m/1800ft; variable surfaces underfoot — you must be sure-footed and agile; possible route-finding problems in poor visibility

● expert — only suitable for very experienced hillwalkers with a head for heights; hazards may include landslides or very narrow trails with no respite from constant exposure

Any of the above grades may be followed by:

❗ *possibility* of vertigo — for those with no head for heights at all
❗❗ ***danger*** of vertigo — you must have a very good head for heights

Over the last few years **waymarking** has improved by leaps and bounds, with many new trails being developed as well. Aside from the nine stages of the 135km-long **GR 131** (waymarked red/white), which runs from the island of Lobos to Punta de Jandía, there are also many shorter walks: **PR**

Hint: On Fuerteventura, the maroon signposts used only for GR routes on other Canary Islands, indicate shorter routes as well! This can be confusing, since the trail signage is very small, in the upper right-hand corner. For instance, this sign is for the green/white waymarked SL FV 29 to Vega de Río Palma.

trails (*'pequenos recorridos'* — day walks, waymarked yellow/white) and **SL trails** (*'senderos locales'* — 'local' walks under 10km long, waymarked green/white). For all routes, horizontal stripes (=) indicate 'continue this way', angled (∠) or right-angled stripes (⌐) show a change of direction; an 'X' (✘) means 'wrong way'.

The **maps** in this book are based on Openstreetmap mapping (see page 2), but have been very heavily annotated from our notes and GPS work in the field. We hope that these maps, which we have found to be *very* accurate on the ground, will be a boon to walkers. It is a pity that we have to reproduce them at only 1:50,000 to keep the book to a manageable size; quite a few walkers buy both the paperback *and* download our pdf files so that they can enlarge the maps (or of course they can be enlarged on a colour photocopier).

Free **GPS track** downloads are available for all these walks: see the Fuerteventura page on the Sunflower website. Please bear in mind, however, that GPS readings should *never* be relied upon as your sole reference point, as conditions can change overnight. *But even if you don't use GPS,* our maps are now so accurate that you can easily compare them with Google Maps on your smartphone and pinpoint your exact position. And it's great fun opening our GPX files in Google Earth to preview the walks in advance!

Where to stay

There are two main resorts: **Corralejo** in the north and **Morro Jable**, with its string of accompanying resorts, in the south. Two lesser resorts are growing apace: **Costa Calma** at the northern end of the Jandía Peninsula, and **Caleta de Fuste** in the centre. The latter offers fairly good bus access to walks at both ends of the island.

Several seaside villages with apartments are also becoming important resorts: El Cotillo, Las Playitas, Gran Tarajal, Tarajalejo, La Lajita, Giniginamar, and La Pared. But remember that finding unreserved accommodation in high season (Christmas through Easter) is difficult.

There are also many **rural hotels and guest houses**, but they no longer have a separate website. Best to search 'rural hotels' on the web.

Puerto del Rosario, the capital, has a few hotels and some *residencias*. Finally, there's also the old *parador,* now in private hands and called 'Hotel Fuerteventura Playa Blanca', just outside Puerto del Rosario.

What to take

If you're already on Fuerteventura when you find this book, and you don't have any special equipment such as walking boots or a rucksack, you can still do some of the walks — or buy yourself some equipment in one of the sports shops. Don't attempt the more difficult walks without the proper gear. For each walk in the book, the *minimum* equipment is listed.

Please bear in mind that I've not done *every* walk in this book under *all* weather conditions. Use your good judgement to modify my list according to the season!

You may find the following checklist useful:

- walking boots
- walking pole(s)
- waterproof rain gear (outside summer months)
- long-sleeved shirt (sun protection)
- bandages and band-aids
- paper plates, cups, etc
- rainwear (zip opening)
- sunhat
- insect repellent
- small rucksack
- up-to-date transport timetables
- lightweight water containers
- extra pair of socks, spare bootlaces
- long trousers, tight at the ankles
- protective sun cream
- knives and openers
- lightweight fleece
- groundsheet
- torch, whistle, compass, GPS
- mobile or smartphone (the emergency number is 112)

Weather

Fuerteventura has a climate to match its beaches: the average temperature is 19°C, with fairly hot summer days and a very mild winter … to say nothing of a healthy 2900+ hours of sunshine per year! But the desert-like climate means that — especially in the north and centre of the island — it can be quite chilly in the evening, *even in summer.*

November to March are the best walking months. Sunseekers, I'm sorry to say that you will get cloudy days, some quite miserable and fresh — just right for a long hike. Wet days — from the blessed (for the islanders) west- to

Beach north of El Cotillo

Walk 7: View over La Oliva to the north, from the Fuente de Tababaire. The mirador *is just ahead (with the panels).*

southwest winds — are quite a phenomenon here; they arrive about as frequently as a real summer in England (when everybody remembers the year…).

The main winds are the northeast to north, which can be very strong all year round — just right for windsurfing and kite-flying, and the bothersome southeast to south *calima* — a dry hot wind off the Sahara that fills the air with dust. These winds can last for up to five days, and are very unpleasant. In summer, mists (from the trade winds) are common over the Jandía mountains, but they won't affect your beach days. So really, all you've got to worry about is the sun and the heat.

Spanish for walkers and motorists

In the tourist centres you hardly need know any Spanish. But out in the countryside, a few words of the language will be helpful, especially if you lose your way. It may also help you 'break through' the natural reserve of the Fuerteventurans.

Here's an — almost — foolproof way to communicate in Spanish. First, memorise the few short key questions and their possible answers, given below. Then, when you have your 'mini-speech' memorised, always ask the many questions you can concoct from it **in such a way that you get a 'sí' (yes) or 'no' answer.** *Never* ask an open-ended question such as 'Where is the main road?'. Instead, ask the question and then suggest the most likely answer yourself. For instance: 'Good day, sir. Please — where is the path to Tindaya? Is it straight ahead?'. Now, unless you get a 'sí' response, try: 'Is it to the left?'. If you go through the list of answers to your own question, you will eventually get a 'sí'

These modern gavias *are seen on Walk 23, above the village of Cardón. In this traditional system of irrigation, land is levelled, then surrounded by metre-high walls of soil (or soil and stone) called* trastones. *Run-off water is sent along canals or pipes into the* gavia, *where it is slowly absorbed, allowing for cultivation. Every* gavia *has an overflow opposite the side where the water comes in: superfluous water is sent on to the next* gavia *or emptied into a barranco.*

response, and this is more reassuring than relying solely on sign language.

Following are the most likely situations in which you may have to practice your Spanish. The dots (…) show where you will fill in the name of your destination. Ask a local person to help you with place name pronunciation.

Walk 16: past the ermita *and shortly before the ruin, we have to decide whether to climb to the Arco de las Peñitas (shown on page 90) or call it a day …*

Asking the way
Key questions

English	Spanish	approximate pronunciation
Good day, sir (madam, miss).	Buenos días, señor (señora, señorita).	**Boo**-eh-nohs **dee**-ahs, sen-**yor** (sen-yor-ah, sen-yor-**ee**-tah).
Please — where is	Por favor — dónde está	**Poor** fah-**vor** — **dohn**-day es-**tah**
the road to …?	la carretera a …?	lah cah-reh-**teh**-rah ah …?
the footpath to…?	la senda de …?	lah **sen**-dah day …?
the way to …?	el camino a …?	el cah-**mee**-noh ah …?
the bus stop?	la parada?	lah pah-**rah**-dah?
Many thanks.	Muchas gracias.	**Moo**-chas **gra**-thee-ahs.

Possible answers

English	Spanish	approximate pronunciation
Is it here?	Está aquí?	Es-**tah** ah-**kee**?
there?	allá?	ayl-**yah**?
straight ahead?	todo recto?	**toh**-doh **rayk**-toh?
behind?	detrás?	day-**tras**?
right?	a la derecha?	ah lah day-**ray**-chah?
left?	a la izquierda?	ah lah eeth-kee-**er**-dah?
above?	arriba?	ah-**ree**-bah?
below?	abajo?	ah-**bah**-hoh?

Asking a taxi driver to take you somewhere and return for you, or asking a taxi driver to meet you at a certain place and time

English	Spanish	approximate pronunciation
Please —	Por favor —	**Poor** fah-**vor** —
take us to …	llévanos a …	l-**yay**-vah-nohs ah…
and return at (place) at (time).*	y venga buscarnos a … a … .*	ee **vain**-gah boos-**kar**-nohs ah (place) ah (time).*

Just point out the time on your watch.

Dogs and other nuisances

With the increase in affluence and corresponding increase in crime on the island, many people now keep **dogs** — not just one dog, but in some cases, two or three. These dogs are there to guard the property, and they do a darned good job of it! I have tried to warn you on walks where you may have problems. Goatherds' dogs are usually all bark and no bite. If dogs worry you, you might like to invest in a 'Dog Dazer' — an easily-portable electronic device which emits a noise inaudible to the human ear but startles aggressive dogs and persuades them to back off. These are easily obtained online.

Usually, where there are goats and sheep, you find **ticks** as well. Fuerteventura is no exception, but because there isn't much long grass on the island, they are less of a nuisance here than elsewhere.

Walk 20: behind the salt pans, you'll see this whale's skeleton — a much photographed focal point in Las Salinas

Organisation of the walks

This book describes hikes and rambles all over the island. To choose a walk that appeals to you, you might begin by looking at the touring map inside the back cover. Here you can see at a glance the overall terrain, the roads, and the location of the walks. Flipping through the book, you will see that there is at least one photograph for every walk.

Having selected one or two potential excursions from the map and the photographs, turn to the relevant walk. At the top of the page you will find planning information: distance/time, grade, equipment, and how to get there. If the grade and equipment are beyond your scope, don't despair! There may be a less demanding short walk — or an easier walk in the same area. If you want a really easy walk, look at the picnic suggestions on pages 11-13.

When you are on your walk, you will find that the text begins with an introduction to the landscape and then turns to a detailed description of the route. The **large-scale maps** (all 1:50,000) have been annotated to show key landmarks. **Times** are given for reaching certain points in the walk. *Note: I am a very fit walker,* and these are 'neat' walking times. If you prefer a more leisurely pace, and you stop to picnic or take photographs, a walk may take you ***more than twice as long.*** Please compare your pace with mine on one or two short walks, before you set off on a long hike.

▬▬▬	main road	♁♁	church, chapel	🌴	palm grove
▬▬▬	secondary road	⊕†	cemetery.cross	𝅃𝅃	pylon.aerial
▭▭▭	dirt road	■	castle, watchtower	**P**	picnic spot (see page 10)
───	jeep track	🚐	bus stop	⊓	picnic tables
-------	footpath	🚗	parking	📷	best views
→2→	route of main walk and direction	♪	spring, tank etc	⌒	cave
→2→	alternative route	**O ❷**	start.waypoint	▯	stadium
→2→	other walk	✶✦	windmill.turbine	⛵	ferry

Walk 1: AROUND LOBOS

Note: You need a (free) permit to visit Lobos, which can be booked at **isladelobos.com** no earlier than 5 days before your visit. The places for each day are divided into two slots, each giving 4 hours' visiting time: morning (recommended, especially in winter, when you will have more hours of light) and afternoon. But in practice no one is checking the permits, and especially in summer, thousands of visitors visit the island.
Distance: 10km/6.2mi; 2h45min
Grade: 🔵 easy, but there is no shade, and it can be hot, windy and dusty. The ascent of Montaña La Caldera is just over 100m/330ft.
Equipment: comfortable walking shoes, fleece, sunhat, suncream, picnic, plenty of water, swimwear
Transport: 🚢 from Corralejo to/from Lobos. There are three boats sailing to Lobos, with different schedules, run by two companies (see page 150). Note that the Visitors' Centre and adjacent WC open immediately after the arrival of the 10.00 ferry and usually close promptly at 15.00. There are no other facilities on the island.

You can have Jandía and El Jable; I'll settle for Lobos any day. A half hour's — sometimes rough — ferry ride with amiable seafarers takes you over to this strange little island of sand and rocky mounds. Seen from Corralejo, Lobos may not even arouse your curiosity. But once you've seen the exquisite lagoon cradled by Casas El Puertito and you've climbed the crater, then finished your day with a dip in the turquoise-green waters off the shore, you'll remember it as

one of the most beautiful spots you've visited. Lobos takes its name from the seals that once inhabited these waters. The island is only 3km off the coast of Fuerteventura and measures just 6.5 sq km.

You follow a track that circles the island. A quad, which belongs to the park rangers, is the only vehicle you'll encounter. On Lobos all the paths and tracks are very clearly marked — *with signs warning you not to leave the marked route: Lobos is a bird sanctuary and a protected area!*

Straight off the JETTY (**❶**), **start out** by heading right, past the VISITORS' CENTRE, to make for the tiny port of Casas El Puertito, a jumble of buildings with a restaurant. A neat wide path leads you there through a landscape dominated by mounds of lava and littered with rock. These small mounds, called *hornitos* ('little ovens'; see photograph caption overleaf) are caused by phreatic eruptions. You'll see the beautiful *Limonium papillatum*, with its paper-like mauve and white flowers. And fluorescent green *tabaiba* glows amidst the sombre rock. You'll also notice plenty of *cosco (Mesembryanthemum nodiflorum)*, the noticeably bright red ice plant, and *Suaeda vera*. A reef of rocky outcrops shelters the lagoon, making it into a perfect natural swimming pool. Through the rock the sand dunes of Corralejo are visible in the background.

Casas El Puertito (**❶**; **7min**) is a picture postcard setting. (Tip: if you want to eat here after your walk, order your meal now: entry to the restaurant at lunch time is only possible with a reservation. Without a reservation, it is possible to buy hot food (if there is any left) or drinks at the window opposite the main entrance to the restaurant — expect to queue! — and take it to the waterside or sit on rocks nearby.

Once past the little houses, continue around the LAGOON. Almost at once, swing back inland and, at a T-junction, head right on the coastal path to **Las Lagunitas** (**❷**), the tidal pools where salt-resistant plants thrive and the habitat of several bird species. *Arthrocnemum fruticosum* (a fern-like plant) grows in the hollows. Ice plants, with transparent papillae resembling water droplets, also catch the attention. This plant

Approaching Playa de la Calera

was once traded for its soda content. The track loops its way through these miniature 'mountains'. The rock is clad in orange and faded-green lichen. Overlooking all this is Montaña La Caldera (the crater), the most prominent feature in this natural park.

Shortly, cross a sandy flat area. The track loops up the embankment; a small fork off to the left cuts the loop and rejoins the track at an INFORMATION BOARD. Lanzarote begins to grow across the horizon. Ignore the forks off to the right (**30min, 37min**). (The second fork leads past a patch of sisal — an aloe-like plant with exceptionally tall flower stems, sheltering in a hollow just a few minutes away.) Soon (**55min**), ignore side-paths to some ugly concrete buildings. Then join a surfaced track coming in from the left.

In a few minutes you're alongside the abandoned building and outhouses of the **Faro de Martiño** (❸; **1h10min**). If you don't plan to climb the crater, this will be your best viewpoint in the walk. You look out over the dark lava hills and the tiny valleys of golden sand that thread their way through them. To the right of the broken-away crater of Montaña La Caldera you'll glimpse Corralejo. Across the straits, just opposite, lie some of Lanzarote's magnificent beaches, from Playa Blanca to Punta Papagayo. (I hope the view inspires you to enjoy a day out on Lanzarote by making the short 25-

Walk 1: Around Lobos

minute ferry crossing and using the notes on pages 130-150 to drive or walk in that island's totally different landscapes.)

From the lighthouse follow the main track (the **GR 131**) off to the right. Within 30 minutes from the lighthouse (at about **1h40min**), you will turn off to climb Montaña La Caldera, by taking the *second* fork off to the right. (But first you might like to take a 30 minute return detour to Caleta del Palo (❸), a beach inside Montaña La Caldera's crater. If so, take the *first* right turn (where a signpost points forwards and backwards, but *not* — at time of writing — to Caleta del Palo) and follow the track along a sandy depression. *Careful: in late spring and early summer breeding seagulls around here can be very aggressive!* You pass a water tank and continue on a path through a narrow 'valley' of rock, which leads down to this black-sand beach. Return the same way.

The signposted **Montaña La Caldera** turn-off comes up four minutes after the detour route. Straight into this track, the route forks. Go right and follow the well-worn, partly cobbled and stepped path that ascends to the RIM OF THE CRATER (❹; **2h10min**). A brilliant sight awaits you. You find yourself on a razor-sharp ridge, looking down sheer walls onto a beach, hidden inside this half-crater. Your vista encompasses the profusion of *hornitos* that make up this island, the dunes of Corralejo, and Fuerteventura's hazy inland hills. To the north, you can trace Lanzarote's coastline as far as Puerto del Carmen. The crater is also home to a large seagull colony. The birds here are apparently used to visitors, as they are not aggressive.

Returning to the GR track, head right. Fifteen minutes after joining the track, watch for the turn-off to the main beach: it comes up two minutes past two concrete buildings that sit in a hollow on your left. This exquisite bay (the recently renamed **Playa de La Calera**; ❺; **2h30min**) is actually a shallow lagoon that curves back deeply into the coastline. Here's where you'll end up passing the rest of the time, no doubt. In fact many people just come over to Lobos to enjoy this beach — it's safe for swimming and one of the settings for Picnic 1.

The hornitos *of Lobos — an intriguing landscape. These phreatic eruptions come about when underground water heats up and expands.*

Montaña La Caldera is home to a large seagull colony: take time to observe the fascinating social behaviour of these beautiful and elegant birds.

Just by the beach, behind a fence, archaeological work has been going on, with the hypothesis that Romans established a seasonal settlement on the islet with the intention of sourcing purple dye from the sea snails found there (purple dye was needed for the clothing of their aristocrats…).

Keep an eye on the departure time of your boat! To return to the ferry, just continue along the track, keeping right at the fork, to return to the JETTY (⊙) at **2h45min**.

Walk 2: FROM CORRALEJO TO EL COTILLO

See also photos on pages 52, 58-59, 60-61, 63
Distance: 22km/13.5mi; 5h20min
Grade: ● easy but very long.
NB: Can be very hot, windy and dusty
Note: There is no large-scale map for this walk because none is needed: just refer to the touring map inside the back cover or whichever island map you are using. (The few waypoints printed in the text are for those using our GPS tracks.) The entire course of the walk can be done in a jeep, since it follows a track. But if you attempt it in your rented car be careful! While the first part is in excellent condition, the second half is sometimes covered in loose sand. Remember the wording of your hire car contract: no venturing off sealed roads is covered by insurance! Note also that a highly-recommended cycle excursion of 28km follows the route Corralejo — Majanicho — Lajares — Corralejo. Avoid cycling on windy days! Cycles are available for hire in Corralejo.
Equipment: stout shoes or sturdy trainers, fleece, sunhat, raingear, suncream, swimwear, picnic, plenty of water
Transport: 🚌 to Corralejo (Lines 06, 08) or 🚗: park near the bus station (28° 44.442'N, 13° 52.271'W). Return on 🚌 from El Cotillo to Corralejo (Line 08), then ongoing 🚌 to Puerto del Rosario if necessary (Line 06)
Shorter walks
1 Popcorn Beach (8.5km/5.3mi; 2h). ● Easy; equipment as above. Access: 🚌 to Corralejo (Lines 06, 08) or 🚗: park near the bus station (28° 44.442'N, 13° 52.271'W). Follow the main walk to **Playa del Bajo de la Burra** ('Popcorn Beach'), with its wild atmosphere and small café, and return the same way.
2 Caleta Beatriz (9km/5.6mi; 2h25min). ● Easy; equipment as above. Access: 🚗 Drive from El Cotillo towards the Faro de El Tostón, but park south of it, by a water cistern (28° 42.685'N, 14° 0.778'W), where the coastal track turns off to the right. *Be warned:* lock everything in the boot; there have been some thefts from cars. Use the touring map to walk to **Caleta Beatriz** and back.

Even though this hike takes little more than five hours, I recommend you make a whole day of it. Leave fairly early before it gets too hot, take lots of swimming breaks, and be in El Cotillo to catch the five o'clock bus back. The last section of the walk will *wow* you with its white sand coves and limpid turquoise waters embraced by dark jagged arms of lava. With civilisation behind you, you head into a no-man's land, crossing a vast sea-plain — at times meandering through rough seas of lava and at times through dunes. Wherever you look, there are stones and rock and plains stretching for miles in all directions. But just when you're getting tired, another alluring cove appears. Do this hike during the week, when there will be less local traffic (mainly surfers). The jeep safaris and 4WD-tourists are unavoidable, but they by no means ruin the walk — or the cycle tour.

50 Landscapes of Fuerteventura

Start out from the BUS STATION (●) in **Corralejo**. Head north down the road to the sea. Just past the bus station, turn left on a motorable dirt track (exit C on the town plan on page 10). Setting out, the most prominent landmark is Bayuyo (Walk 3), the volcanic cone on the left with a gaping crater. Ascending slightly, you have an uninterrupted view of Lanzarote and its built-up coastline. Playa Blanca is the resort directly across from you. And back to your right is the little 'pimply' island of Lobos (Walk 1), littered with small volcanic mounds. On the left side of the track you look out over *'malpais'* (badlands) lava … and are soon swallowed up in it. Stone walls in varying stages of decay criss-cross this landscape, and volcanic cones rise out of it. Apart from succulents and small thorny bushes *(aulaga)*, little other vegetation survives here. Rock and stones cover the ground. The landscape appears dark and subdued, until a closer look at the *malpais* reveals varying shades of green lichen plastered across it, and the jagged rock is a mass of turbulent humps and hollows.

In **1h** or less you arrive at **Playa del Bajo de la Burra**, familiarly known as 'Popcorn Beach'. You're bound to be intrigued by the 'sand' here — it looks exactly like puffed-up popcorn (see photo opposite)! It's composed of originally red marine plants called 'rodoliths', bleached by the sea and washed up onto the beach. There was a small café on this beach when we last visited, another reason for a short break.

Right: a sign warns people not to take the 'popcorn' (top), Majanicho (middle), and approaching the Faro de El Tostón

You'll pass a few lone fishermen's shacks; then, at **1h50min** more or less, a small rustic settlement comes up. Crossing a rise, **Majanicho**, which still about 15 minutes away, comes into sight. This retreat of little weekend houses encircles a narrow shallow inlet with a small sandy beach. Unfortunately, on our last visit, there was no bar/café, but there *was* a slight smell of algae — perhaps emanating from Majanicho's 'popcorn'. At **2h05min** a road branches off left for Lajares (❶; the cycle route) and the large tourist development of El Jablito; keep straight ahead.

Beyond Majanicho the terrain briefly becomes sandy, and you pass behind another beach. This is a popular surfing spot, but the beach itself is very rocky, hence no good for swimming. Just past the

Ayuntamiento de
La Oliva
LLEVARSE RODOLITOS DE LA PLAYA
OWED TO TAKE RHODOLITHS WITH YOU
THEY ARE NOT POP-CORN ...
LEAVE THEM IN YOUR HABITAT

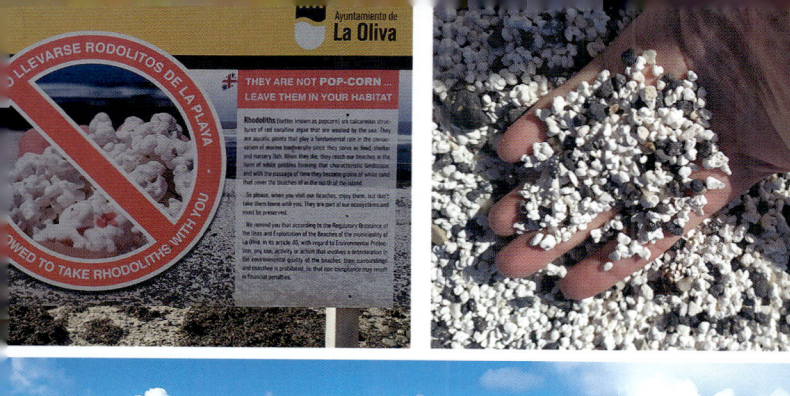

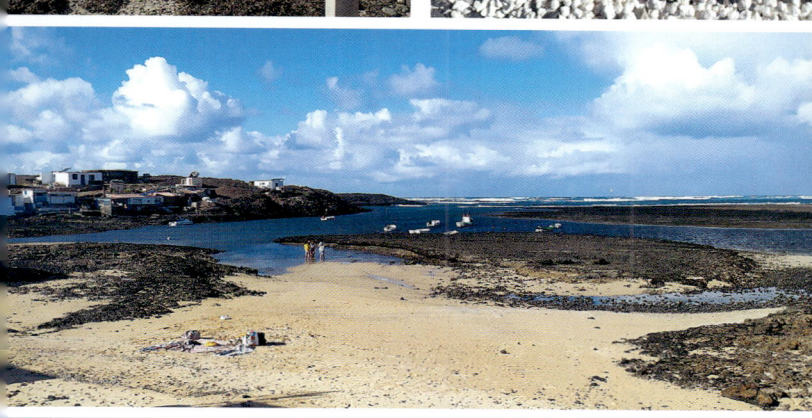

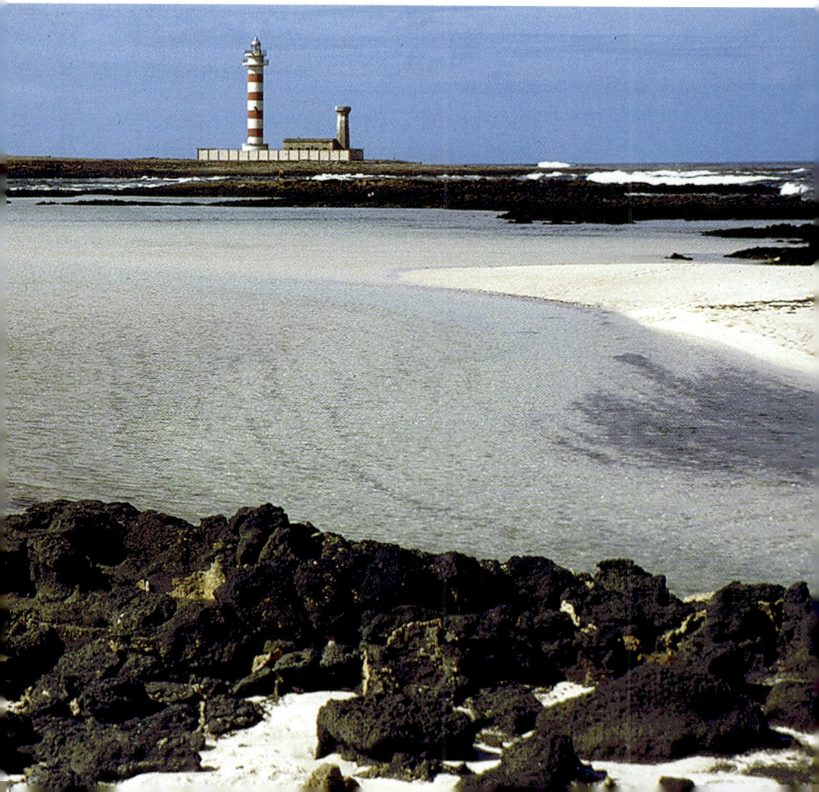

Playa del Castillo, just south of El Cotillo

beach a short ascent gives you a bird's-eye view back over it — and there's still time to change your mind if you think I have underestimated it. My favourite swimming spot lies a little further on. Just before it, you pass a smaller inlet with a couple of beach shanties — also a nice swimming spot.

The track circles behind *my* beach, **Caleta Beatriz** (❷), at **3h15min** into the walk. It's the deepest of the inlets so far. The water is an irresistible green, and there's a nice slab of sand at the end of it. Moreover, nobody seems to stop here. The next bay seems more popular — perhaps because it's not quite so close to the track. The lighthouse at Punta de Tostón is now an obvious landmark.

Nearly an hour further on, a biggish bay (**Caleta del Marrajo**; ❸) stretches across in front of you, with the lighthouse at the far side. It's a beautiful stretch of coastline. Jagged arms of rock jut out into the bay, creating lagoon-like pools. Sand dunes roll back inland. If the track forks behind the bay, keep right, along the shore. Towards the end of the bay the track climbs towards a stone water cistern just beyond which you reach the ROAD FROM EL COTILLO TO THE LIGHTHOUSE (**4h20min**).

Turning left, follow this road, using track short-cuts. Coming into **El Cotillo**, keep straight on along Avenida Los Lagos until you reach a T-junction. Turn left here for 100m, then cross the Lajares road and continue straight ahead (at the right of La Cantina de Fragiel). After 150m you reach the BUS STATION on your right (❹; **5h20min**).

Walk 3: THE CRATER ROUTE

Distance: 12km/7.4mi; 2h55min
Grade: 🔵 easy-moderate; ascent of 160m/525ft — or 🔴 including the detour to Bayuyo (another 150m/490ft of ascent and 40min)
Equipment: comfortable walking shoes, light jacket, sunhat, raingear, suncream, picnic, plenty of water
Refreshments: café in Lajares; bars and restaurants in Corralejo
Transport: 🚐 to Lajares (Lines 7, 8); return on 🚐 from Corralejo (Lines 7, 8)

Shorter walk: Calderón Hondo (8km/5mi; 2h15min). 🔵 grade/equipment as above. 🚗 to/from Lajares: park by the stadium (28° 40.807'N, 13° 55.940'W) or at the start of the SL FV 2 (28° 41.346'N, 13° 55.891'W); 🚐 as above. Follow the main walk to **Calderón Hondo** and the HERDERS' CORRALS (❷). Back at the turn-off to the viewpoint, take the path to the right, unmarked but well trodden. Turn left downhill after 150m.

This hike along the Bayuyo alignment of volcanic craters is one of the most fascinating walks in the Canaries — and especially worthwhile if you've not been to Lanzarote or done the Ruta de los Volcanes on La Palma. Those of you interested in vulcanology will have a field day. And even if you couldn't give a hoot about volcanoes, it's *still* a brilliant walk — especially early in the evening under the setting sun.

Start out from the BUS STOP (🔴) in **Lajares** next to the FOOTBALL GROUND. Head north on the road at the right of this stadium (CALLE MAJANICHO). Follow this road for 10 minutes (1km). Then, just past the last house on the right, turn off right on the wide, green/white waymarked **SL FV 2** footpath signposted 'CALDERON HONDO'.

Your way is exquisitely cobbled and bordered by stones on both sides — a work of art. Surrounded by a lichen-covered *malpais,* ignore an unmarked path to the left (the return route for the short walk) and head straight towards a dark reddish-brown volcanic mound, **Montaña Colorada**, which rises boldly in front of you. The path skirts the foot of this volcano to the right (white/green waymark),

Setting off on the walk, with Montaña Colorada in the background. Many paths on the island are as beautifully 'manicured' as this one.

Calderón Hondo, shown above (with Montaña Colorada and Lajares behind it), is one of several craters that erupted at the same time about 50,000 years ago. Theses eruptions actually added over 100 sq km to the island's northern land mass — and created the island of Lobos as well. This walk takes in the 5km Bayuyo alignment on Fuerteventura itself, heading northeast via Colorada, Hondo, Rebanada, Encantada, Caldera, and Bayuyo. This last volcano, which gives its name to the alignment, comes from one of the pre-Hispanic tribes which inhabited the island in days past.

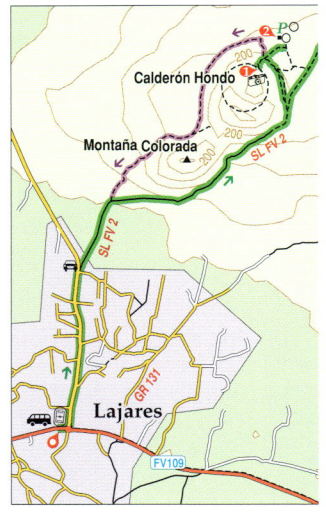

then ascends to an elevated plain. Magnificent stone walls stretch across the inclines below. The next volcanic mound to appear on the left is Calderón Hondo. Crossing a crest, you pass through a wall. To the right you look out over the sand dunes of Corralejo, separating the dark lava flow and the blue sea.

On coming to a fork at the base of **Calderón Hondo** (**50min**), head uphill to the left. After five minutes ignore two paths forking off to the right very close together; continue steeply uphill to the left, to the VIEWPOINT (**❶**; **1h02min**). An impressive crater lies 70 metres below the perfectly circular rim shown above. A surprising amount of vegetation grows on and out of the rock here. You have excellent sea views both left and right. Majanicho is the small seaside

Recommended detours: Ten minutes after the Cotos Tamboriles junction, a short path to the left leads to the **Cueva Natural** (**a**), a hole in the lava caused by a volcanic gas bubble. Some 150m past the 'bubble path' a cairn-marked path heads right and climbs to the summit of **Bayuyo**. After 20 minutes you reach the top of the lower ridge, 10 minutes more take you to the TRIG POINT (**b**). Ignore the path down off to the right from here; go left along the ridge for about 200m to the clear but steep and at times skiddy descent path. At the bottom of the mountain, go left and left again, back to the track where you can pick up the notes below. Allow 40 minutes extra for this detour.

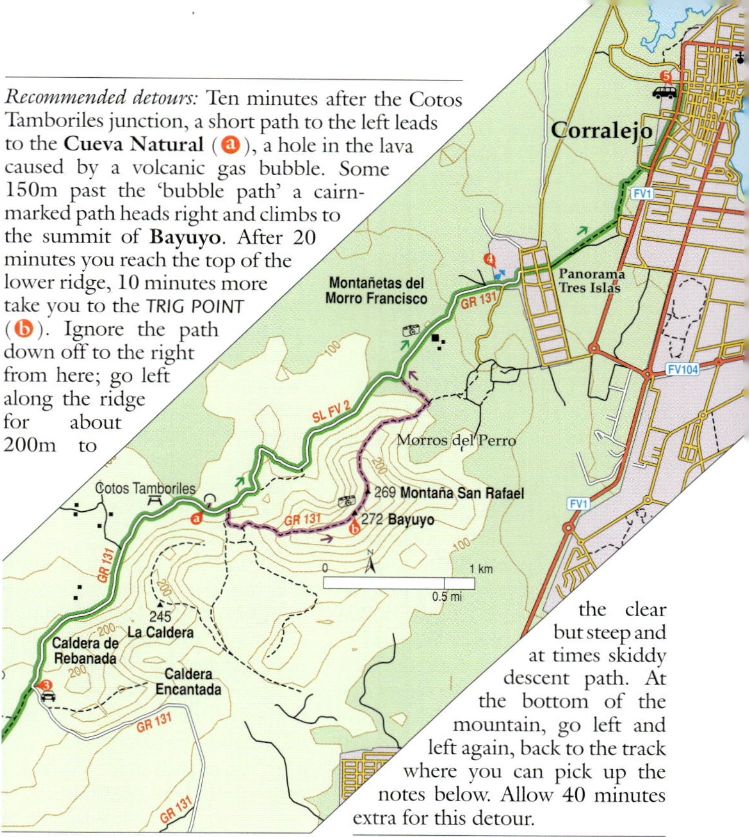

village seen to the left. The plains below are littered with corrals and dotted with buildings, many of which lie abandoned.

Now head back to the two forks you passed on your way to the *mirador*: they are now descending on your left. Take the second turning. *(The Shorter walk will descend to Lajares at the first*

This replica herders' hut on Calderón Hondo, with its thatch and mud roof, supporting beams and lava stone walls, paints a vivid picture of the past.

turning.) Minutes along, you come to a traditional HERDERS' STONE BUILDING (❷). The small stone conical construction to the right was used for cooking. Nearby is a corral, also made of lava stone.

Return to the point where you turned off to the *mirador,* and now head left towards Corralejo. Crossing this elevated plain, you look into **Caldera de Rebanada**, the collapsed crater on your right. Five minutes later, a dirt road (the GR 131) cuts across in front of you, by a car park (❸). Follow the road to the left downhill towards the scattered dwellings of **Cotos Tamboriles**. Ignore the turn-off left to this hamlet and continue straight on towards Corralejo. You can now ignore all turnings and just follow the road along the foot of the volcanoes *(but see the note on the preceding page, beside the map)*.

La Caldera, another prominent volcanic cone, overshadows you on the right. Heading into an undulating landscape of lava, the way now ascends, and you twist and wind through hillocks and depressions. Amidst the stone and rock there's a surprising amount of greenery about in spring — if the island's been blessed with the normal February rains.

Forty minutes along the road, you cross a crest and dip into the gaping crater of **Bayuyo** (**2h05min**), a landmark for miles around Corralejo. This amphitheatre of mountain is about to encompass you when your way swings off left. You pass some abandoned sheds and stables and one or two illegal tips. Soon after, rounding a bend in the hillside, Corralejo comes into sight (but it's not as close as it looks!) … and a corner of Lobos.

Descending, and out of the lava, you pass a large white WATER TANK (❹) on the left and come to a crossing road at a lone housing estate (**Panorama Tres Islas**) with few properties. Cross straight over to the far side of the estate, then follow the dirt road through a grim wasteland. It approaches the main road, then a path moves away to the left before joining the main dual carriageway again (Avenida Juan Carlos I). Turn left for 10 minutes, to **Corralejo**'s BUS STATION (❺; **2h55min**), on the left.

Corralejo comes into sight (but it's not as close as it looks!) … with Lobos to the right. Across the sea, Lanzarote's Ajache Mountains rise to the east of Playa Blanca.

Walk 4: FUENTES DE EL CHUPADERO

Distance: 3.6km/2.3mi; 1h30min
Grade: ● fairly easy ascent/descent of 230m/755ft on a well built path. Not waymarked, but easily followed
Equipment: walking shoes, walking pole(s), fleece, sunhat, suncream, raingear in winter, picnic, water
Transport: 🚗 to/from the walkers' info board on the FV10, 350m west of the bar/restaurant in La Matilla (28° 33.809'N, 13° 57.582'W). Or 🚐 (Line 07) to La Matilla, then on foot to the start

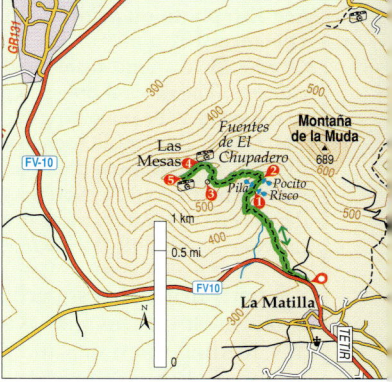

It doesn't have an official number yet, but this pleasant, fairly easy trail past three springs and culminating in a fine viewpoint on Montaña de la Muda has recently been laid out by the island government.

Start out west of **La Matilla** at the large WALKERS' INFORMATION BOARD (○) by going up the wide stepped path shown below, rising past abandoned terracing and a number of old stone shelters. At the side of the path signs indicate the local and botanical names of some of the plants on view in this area. Before long, a right turn leads to the first spring, 20m away (**Fuente del Risco**; ❶; **15min**). Pretty **Fuente de la Pila** is just above it at the left. A shelter and primitive barbecue pit (without any wood…) sit above the third spring (**Fuente del Pocito**; ❷). These springs don't run dry even in summer.

The higher you climb, the better the view. Now you overlook the Tefía plain and the Betancuria massif behind it — setting for Walks 12-14. From the shelter the path runs along the flanks of **Montaña de la Muda**. You pass an old threshing floor (*era*; ❸) and rise up to a ridge, **Las Mesas** (❹; **45min**). From here you look out over northern Fuerteventura and over to Lobos and Lanzarote. But continue for another five minutes to a CAIRN (❺; **50min**). Now the view takes in more of the island's northwest, including Montaña Tindaya.

The ascent to the summit of Muda is only suitable for experienced climbers with a guide, so retrace your steps from here back to the WALKERS' INFORMATION BOARD (○; **1h30min**).

Wide steps beside the FV10 at the start of the walk

Walk 5: CLIFFTOP WALK FROM EL COTILLO

See also photo on page 52
Distance: 10km/6.2mi: 3h
Grade: 🔵 easy, mostly along the clifftops. The descent down steps to the sea may be unnerving for some. *Note:* don't walk too close to the cliff- edge, it could crumble away beneath you! And on windy days keep even further away from the edge of the cliffs. *No shade.*

Equipment: comfortable walking shoes, swimming things, fleece, sunhat, raingear, suncream, picnic, plenty of water
Transport: 🚗 to El Cotillo: park at the watchtower, Torre de El Tostón (28° 40.807'N, 14° 0.623'W). Or 🚌 to/from El Cotillo (Lines 07, 08): head for the coast and turn left to the tower.

Apart from the superb sea views, what delighted me most on this hike were the barbary ground squirrels. Yes, feeding them bits and pieces from my lunch. Doing just the kind of thing they ask you *not* to do in the parks, where the signs all read 'please don't feed the squirrels'.

View west from the opposite the fishing port in El Cotillo, just north of the Torre de El Tostón

Walk 5: Clifftop walk from El Cotillo

The hike starts from the 17th-century WATCHTOWER (**Torre de El Tostón**; (○)). It's currently being restored as a tourist information centre, where contemporary art exhibitions are also held. From the tower you overlook a long sandy beach that rests at the foot of dunes. Beyond the beach rise sheer cliffs. The hike will take you along this beach, before you mount the cliffs and head along them. No matter what time of day you start out, you'll see surfers out on the waves.

Follow the track behind the tower, heading south. A couple of minutes along, at a fork, descend the crest and start making your way along the beach. On windy days, which are common, sand gets blown into every orifice! (*Always remember*: the beaches on this side of the island are dangerous because of undertows. People do swim at this beach, but *don't* venture out far.)

When you reach the END OF THE BEACH (**30min**) climb to the clifftops above. Now up on the sea-plain, just follow the faint track traced out along the top. It's part of the **PR FV 1** followed in Walk 6; we join this trail at **Punta Mallorquín** (❶; **40min**). Looking back, you can see El Cotillo across from you, and inland, the small village of El Roque. Apart from a few lone buildings, there is little sign of life inland. Smooth denuded hills rise off the plain.

The coastline with its sheer cliffs

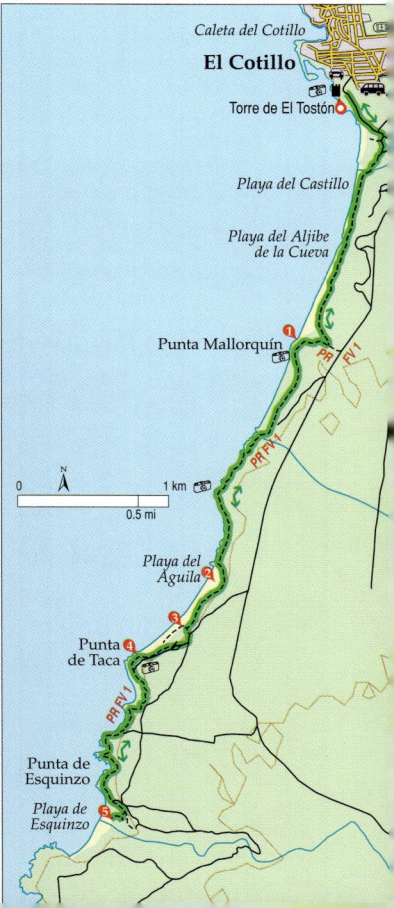

60 Landscapes of Fuerteventura

keeps your attention. Below, you can see a shelf of submerged rock extending quite far out into the aquamarine sea. Within **1h** you're overlooking a big bite in the shoreline — the long sweep of **Playa del Aguila** (❷). From the clifftop here look towards the cliffs in the latter half of the 'bite', and you should be able to see steps down to the sea — your immediate destination. Some minutes further along, a small sandy beach appears at the foot of the cliffs below.

A little over 10 minutes later, you're at the top of the STEPS (❸; **1h15min**). Just before you descend, you have a beautiful view back along the coastline to El Cotillo, and in the distance you can see the lighthouse at Punta de Tostón. Some people may find the descent unnerving, but these concrete steps are very sound. Beyond the stones at the foot of the steps, you can see the sandy seabed. The sea looks very tranquil, and it's quite shallow. I've never swum here, nor have I seen others do so, so take extra care if

You needn't go looking for the barbary ground squirrels — they'll find you!

you do try these waters. (If you want to walk to the small beach overlooked earlier, it lies 10 minutes along to the right — *but if you walk there, keep your eye on the tides.*) This is also where you'll find the squirrels ... on the clifftops and along the rocky shoreline. (You needn't find them, they'll find you!)

Climb back up the steps and, before heading back to the watchtower, walk along to the right for 10 minutes — over to the next small headland, **Punta de Taca** (❹; **1h40min**), where you'll find a well-placed bench overlooking another fine sea view. From here the main walk retraces steps to **El Cotillo** (**O**; **3h**), but if you've another hour or so in hand, why not continue along the the cliffs to the information board where the PR FV 1 ends, at **Playa de Esquinzo** (❺)?

Looking back to El Cotillo from Playa del Castillo

Walk 6: CAÑADA DE MELIAN

See also photos on pages 2, 50-51, 52, 58-59, 60-61
Distance: 7.8km/4.8mi; 2h20min
Grade: ● easy, with an ascent of 100m/320ft and descent of 140m/460ft. Signposted and yellow/white waymarked PR FV 1
Equipment: comfortable walking shoes, swimming things, fleece, sunhat, raingear, suncream, picnic, plenty of water
Transport: 🚐 to/from the walkers' signpoard for the PR FV 1 just past KM31 heading west from Lajares on the FV10 (28° 40.920'N, 13° 57.360'W). Or 🚐 (Lines 07, 08) to Lajares, then walk 1.7km to the start. Return on 🚐 from El Cotillo, back to Lajares (Line 08) or back to base (Lines 07, 08)
Alternative walk: Playa de Esquinzo (21km/13mi; 5h15min).
● Moderate on account of the length; equipment/transport as main walk. *Highly recommended if you've missed Walk 5.* Follow the main walk from (⊙) to **El Cotillo** (**❺**), then use the notes/map on pages 58-61 to follow Walk 5 to **Playa de Esquinzo** where the PR FV 1 ends (or just go part-way). Then retrace steps.

You follow the white-sand Cañada de Melián south in an utterly peaceful but very dry setting. The Majada de las Pilas, some 3km along, is a semi-desert plain which hosts some of the most interesting desert bird life on the island. If you're lucky, you may even see a road runner — the *hubara canaria,* symbol of the island.

Start out at the WALKERS' SIGNBOARD FOR THE **PR FV 1** just west of KM31 on the FV10 (⊙). Ignore several tracks towards the **Montaña de la Mareta** off to the right. The *cañada* splits but both arms rejoin after a few hundred metres. Underfoot you're sure to spot small white/grey 'stones' with holes at one end like the ones shown opposite: they're PETRIFIED WASPS' NESTS. After 20 minutes or so you pass some strange brick structures on the right.

When the river beds splits again at a signpost for 'EL COTILLO' (**❶**; **40min**), turn right alongside a fence, into another wide river bed. Pass some very large earthen walls on your right, and a few minutes later turn right on a well marked track. At the **Majada de las Pilas**

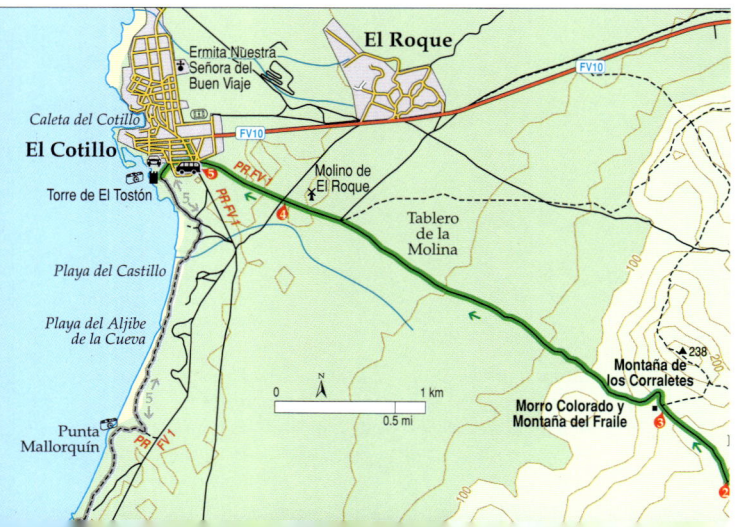

Walk 6: Cañada de Melián 63

Heading off on the wide cañada *at the start of the walk; below: petrified wasps' nests; the port at El Cotillo, with the Torre de El Tostón on the headland*

(❷; **1h**) an information board points out different species of desert birds that can be seen in this area. Ascending northeast, you pass **Montaña de los Corraletes** and a SHELTER (❸; **1h15min**). Then, as you start descending, you have Montaña del Fraile to the left and El Cotillo and the little village of El Roque ahead.

Once past the few houses on the slopes of **Montaña del Fraile**, you come to another plain, the **Tablero de la Molina**. Fifty minutes later you cross a MAJOR TRACK (❹; **2h05min**); the attractive lone windmill shown on page 2 is just 200m to the right. Continue straight on to the BUS STATION at **El Cotillo** (❺; **2h20min**) — or join Walk 5 and head south along the coast.

Walk 7: FROM TINDAYA TO LA OLIVA

See photos on pages 4, 12, 35, 40
Distance: 8.8km/5.5mi; 3h20min
Grade: 🔴 ∷ moderate-strenuous ascent/descent of 220m/700ft. The 15-minute pathless descent from the *mirador* is very steep and skiddy; you must be sure-footed and have a head for heights. Partly signposted and yellow/white waymarked PR FV 9
Equipment: hiking boots, walking poles, light jacket, sunhat, raingear, suncream, picnic, plenty of water
Transport: 🚌 to Tindaya; park by the church (28° 35.172'N, 13° 58.689'W). Or 🚐 to Tindaya (Line 07); alight at the bus shelter by the church. Return on 🚐 from La Oliva (Lines 07, 08), back to your car at Tindaya (Line 07) or back to base

Short walk: Fuente and Mirador de Tababaire from Vallebrón (5km/3mi; 1h20min). 🔵 Easy-moderate, with a steady climb of 100m/330ft; comfortable shoes will suffice. 🚌 to/from the Centro Socio Cultural in Vallebrón (28° 34.939'N, 13° 56.036'W). No bus service. Follow 'Tindaya' signs from there to ❸; then, ignoring an 'X' on the track, fork *right* to ❹ (the *mirador* and *fuente*). Return the same way. Note that you could also turn *left* at ❸; then, from ❷, take a good path up to the telecoms aerial and on to ❹.

T he hidden Valle Chico that cradles Vallebrón is very little visited… and the *mirador* on this walk is one of the best on the island, yet hardly anyone knows about it … except for a few jeep safaris.

Start the walk from the BUS STOP/CAR PARKING by the CHURCH in **Tindaya** (⭕), where there is a WALKERS' INFORMATION BOARD. Head east on CALLE LA OLIVA following the signposted **PR FV 9**. Just before reaching the FV10 road, the trail turns left on a signposted dirt track parallel with the road. Ignore a first tunnel on the right but, five minutes later, a fingerpost (missing when last checked) should guide you under the FV10 via a SECOND TUNNEL (❶; **30min**).

The path is now stone-lined for a short while, then turns right towards the mountains, twice crossing a gully. A log-stepped path takes you up to a SADDLE (❷; **1h**) between **Morro de Tababaire** in the north and **Montaña de Enmedio** in the south — with a fine view back towards Montaña Tindaya rising in splendid isolation from the plain.

From the saddle continue east on a dirt track, passing old fields, descending into **Valle Chico**. Below you lies the sleepy, pretty village of Vallebrón. Keep to this track until you come to a T-JUNCTION with a wider, motorable track a couple of hundred metres short of the first houses of **Vallebrón**. Turn left here (❸; **1h15min**). *(The Short walk joins here.)* You will now keep to this direct road all the way to the

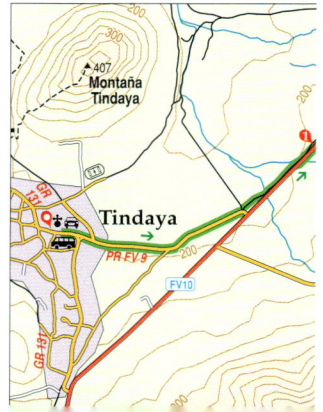

Walk 7: From Tindaya to La Oliva 65

mirador. You pass — and *smell* — a GOAT/SHEEP/PIG FARM with lots of animals on the loose on the track and the surrounding mountainside. Montaña Tindaya and its surrounding village creep into view again as you ascend.

Around 30 minutes up the track, pass a fork off left to a TELECOMMUNICATIONS AERIAL (**1h45min**). (If you take this 15 minute detour, you will be rewarded with a fine outlook over Tindaya and surroundings.) Then a spectacular view unravels. La Oliva, a small farming settlement, sits in the middle of a patchwork of fields. An ochre and black volcanic cone called La Arena stands boldly behind it. And on a clear day this superb panorama is made complete with Lanzarote filling the background, and a deep blue sea stretching to the horizon. A little further on, when you get to the *mirador*, you will be able to sit down and just soak it all up. The motorable gravel track ends at the **Fuente de Tababaire** (**4**; **2h05min**), a couple of small water troughs cut into the rock face — a water source for animals. The **Mirador de Tababaire** (also called Mirador de la Degollada de Valle Grande) is just a minute further on. *(The Short walk turns back here.)* There is a sort of 'table d'orientation' at the *mirador*, pointing out the various landmarks, and a telescope for a closer view.

To continue the main walk, hold your breath and take your bearings: you now make your own way down this very steep hillside, pathless, first aiming for the LARGE SALMON-COLOURED FARM straight below the *mirador*. At the bottom of the mountain, turn right alongside the surrounding ANIMAL FENCE (**5**; **2h20min**). Cross several gullies and when you come to the CORNER OF THE FENCE (**6**; **2h40min**), skirt to the right of it — again pathless, outside the fence — until you meet a TRACK (**7**; **3h05min**).

Follow this to the left, past the school and into **La Oliva**. A BUS SHELTER (**8**; **3h20min**) is on the main road by the CHURCH, opposite a PHARMACY. You pass roads to the Casa de los Coroneles, which is worth a visit if you've not been there before (see photo on page 12 and history on page 34).

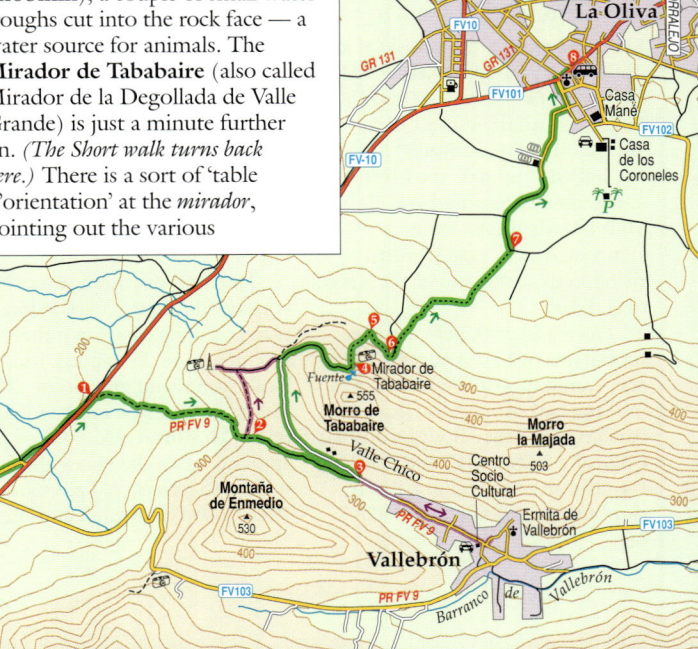

Walk 8: FROM TETIR TO TEFIA

Distance: 12.8km/7.9mi; 4h10min
Grade: 🔴❗ moderate-strenuous, with an overall ascent of 360m/1180ft and descent of 435m/1425ft; the ascent from Tetir and the descent to Casillas del Angel is on sometimes narrow and exposed mountain trails. Signposted and yellow/white waymarked PR FV 15
Equipment: hiking boots, walking poles, fleece, sunhat, raingear, suncream, picnic, plenty of water
Transport: 🚌 to Tetir; park near the church (28° 31.912'N, 13° 55.139'W). Or 🚐 to Tetir (Line 07); alight at the 'Iglesia Tetir' stop on the FV10 and walk 220m to the church. Return on 🚐 from Tefía (Line 02) and change buses in Puerto del Rosario if necessary to return to your car.

Alternative walk: Circuit from Casillas del Angel (15.3km/9.5mi; under 5h). 🔴❗ Grade as main walk, but the overall ascent/descent is about 600m/1970ft. Equipment as main walk. Access by 🚌 or 🚐 to Casillas del Angel; park near the restaurant/supermarket 50m inland of the FV10 (28° 29.607'N, 13° 58.114'W), 120m west of the bus stop, and start the walk at (❺). Allow an *extra* 1.2km/20min return to detour into Tefía and 4.5km/1h10min to detour into Tetir.

Tetir is an unpretentious small agricultural village but with an impressive feature: the enormous *gavias* (see page 41) surrounding this village. The walk takes you along a number of them, before climbing up onto a ridge and giving you magnificent views over a large part of the island. In the hills you'll see plenty of goats and sheep and on the crests hear and see ravens and buzzards. This walk and Walk 9 are ideal for those travelling by bus; for motorists the Alternative walk is more suitable — there are no logistical problems getting back to your car by bus.

Start the walk at the CHURCH in **Tetir**, by a WALKERS' INFO BOARD for the **PR FV 15**, 'VALLE DE TETIR' (❍): head southwest out of the village on CALLE DOMINGO JUAN MANRIQUE. You pass the CEMETERY and a salmon-coloured WRESTLING STADIUM, then turn left on a PR-signposted track (❶; **15min**), rising in the company of fine views over Tetir.

From a SADDLE between the mountains of **San Andrés** (left) and **Tamateje** (right), head down into the barren valley of Tetir, reaching the valley floor by an OLD FARM at a SIGNPOSTED CROSSROADS (❷; **35min**). Go straight ahead, climbing the hillside to a HIKERS' SHELTER (❸) with an INFO BOARD about the geology in this area. From here a stony stepped path leads you to the top of the ridge at the **Degollada de la Sargenta** (❹; **1h10min**). The valley that cradles Casillas del Angel lies at your feet; to the left is the ocean beyond the airport.

The descent path now narrows considerably and is exposed in places as it zigzags down the mountainside. It's skiddy, too, with loose stones and grit. Some 20 minutes down you cross an old track (**1h30min**). As you approach the valley floor the path widens to a track and passes a SHEEP FARM on the left and then an

Walk 8: From Tetir to Tefía

OLIVE PLANTATION on the right — the latter a new agricultural project for Fuerteventura: the island is now producing ecological olive oil!

A larger track joins yours, then you come on to a signposted road (**2h15min**); at the fork that follows, turn right. Turn right again just 50m short of the main FV20 road in **Casillas del Angel** and pass two BARS/RESTAURANTS (⑤) and a SUPERMARKET. *(Those doing the Alternative walk can park here, or walk here from the bus stop.)* Keep ahead past the market. The road, waymarked yellow/white, becomes a track (ignore all turn-offs), rising to the saddle ahead. At a Y-fork by a WIRE MESH FENCE, go right, with the fence on your right. Reaching a saddle, the **Degollada de la Vista de Casillas** (⑥; **3h 10min**), you have fine views over Llanos de la Concepción (Walk 11), and to the far left you can see the Morro Velosa *mirador* and the area of Walks 13 and 14.

Walk along the crest to the right; now you look down on the Puertito de Los Molinos area, where Walk 10 starts and ends. Five minutes later you pass a WOODEN CROSS at a place called **Reposa Duelos** ('mourners' rest'). In times gone by there was no graveyard in Tefía, so when somebody died the coffin had to be carried over this mountain trail to Casillas del Angel for burial. As it was the highest point, the funeral cortège stopped here to rest.

Just past the cross the trail turns left down the mountainside and Tefía is visible — another tiny village. Almost immediately, you meet another trail and continue to the right. As you round the

Below: on the descent to Tetir; right: Reposa Duelos

The pretty Ermita de San Augustín at Tefía makes a lovely picnic spot.

hillside, Montaña Tindaya (see pages 33-34) peeks out between two other mountains in the north. Continue on the stone-lined path crossing several dry water courses. At a SIGNPOSTED JUNCTION (**7**; **3h 45min**) turn right. Another junction follows: keep right here as well. A few minutes later you pass the CHURCH (**8**; **4h**) and CULTURAL CENTRE in **Tefía**. *(For the Alternative walk, turn right just past the church — or allow 30 minutes return to take a look around Tefía.)* Continue down to the main FV207 road, heading right at two Y-forks; a BUS SHELTER (**9**; **4h10min**) is some 30m to the right, opposite a restaurant.

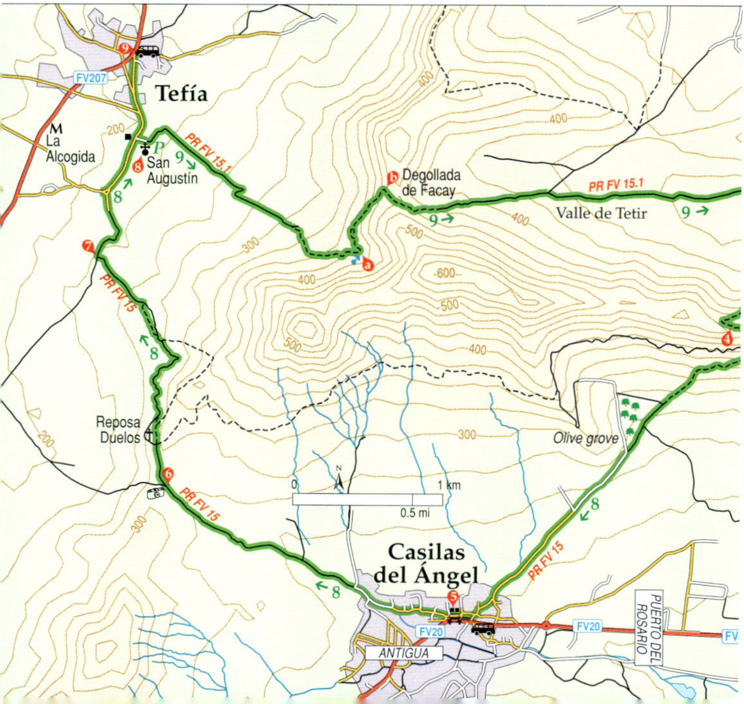

Walk 9: FROM TEFIA TO TETIR

See photo opposite
Distance: 8km/5mi; 2h50min
Grade: 🔴❗ easy to moderate, with an overall ascent of about 300m/1000ft (some exposed paths); yellow/white waymarked PR FV 15.1
Equipment: as Walk 8, page 66
Transport: 🚍 to Tefía; park near the FV207 bus shelter (28° 31.657'N, 13° 59.377'W). Or 🚐 to Tefía (Line 02). Return on 🚐 from Tetir (Line 07), changing in Puerto del Rosario if necessary to return to your car.
Longer walk: See the Alternative walk on page 66.

Tefía is a one-horse town (possibly a one-camel town...), but just south of it on the FV207 is La Alcogida, a beautifully presented open-air ecomuseum of houses and other features of agricultural life in the past.

Start out facing the BUS SHELTER (**9**) on the main FV207 in **Tefía**. Take the road about 30m to the right of it, *not* the road directly opposite the restaurant. Turn left just before the pretty old **Ermita de San Augustín** (**8**; **10min**) on a signposted track which quickly heads towards the mountains.

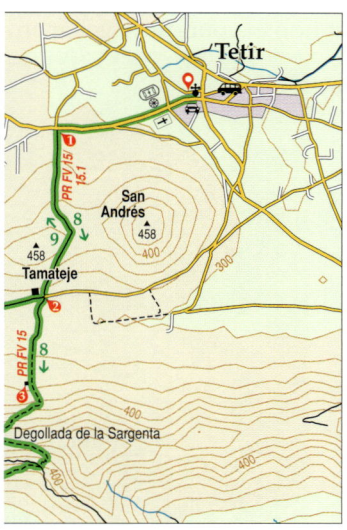

Meeting a fence, follow it to the right past a SHEEP/GOAT FARM with yapping dogs (**35min**); then the path climbs alongside the fence and narrows.

Beyond the fence, keep up this well defined but skiddy path. In a dip in the mountainside you come to two small SPRINGS (**a**; **55min**), where you may see a flock of ravens happily enjoying the water. Now the path narrows again, with a steep drop to the left... and fine views over Tefía and Llanos de la Concepción. Reaching a SADDLE (**Degollada de Facay**; **1h15min**; **b**), you look all the way down Tetir's wide open valley to the village.

Start down on the clear path to your right — the PILGRIMS' ROUTE to the Virgin of La Peña in Vega de Río Palmas. You cross a few steep gullies on rough-hewn bridges. Abandoned fields lie left and right, but some goat pens seem to be still in business.

Keep right at a SIGNPOSTED JUNCTION. At a SIGNPOSTED CROSSROADS by an OLD FARM (**2**; **2h05min**), turn left uphill on track. Ten minutes later you're on the crest, with **Tetir** at your feet. Descend to a road (**1**) and turn right to the CHURCH and BAR. Pass them and take the next left, to the main road: a BUS SHELTER (**0**; **2h50min**) is just to the left.

Walk 10: PUERTITO DE LOS MOLINOS CIRCUIT

Distance: 8.4km/5.2mi; 2h25min
Grade: 🔵 relatively easy, with a small climb out of a *barranco* and then cross-country. Mostly on tracks and well defined footpaths. No waymarking (although there are a few cairns), but easily followed
Equipment: stout walking shoes, walking pole(s), light jacket, sunhat, suncream, raingear in winter, picnic, water
Transport: 🚗 to Puertito de los Molinos (28° 32.556'N, 14° 3.791'W); note that sometimes on weekends the restaurants get very busy, so make sure your car is not blocked from leaving!
Note: Before setting off on the walk, you may want to have a look at the rugged coastline by following a well-defined path on the left side of the port for 50 metres, to where it ends on the rocks at a viewpoint. *Take care; the coast is brittle and can be dangerous.*
Short walk: Barranco de los Molinos (either 4km/2.5mi; 1h15min if you park at ○ or 1.3km/under half a mile if you park at ❺; in either case, allow extra time for bird-watching). 🔵 Very easy; access and equipment as the main walk. Follow the stone-lined trail from Puertito de los Molinos to the hide, or approach it from the car park on the track west of Las Parcelas.

Laid-back Puertito de Los Molinos, with its handful of fishing shacks and two small restaurants, lies at one end of a bird sanctuary. A squabble of ducks have taken up residence in the pools below the first restaurant; hang on to your picnic — they will all but hop in your car to get at any food! The evergreen gorge opening out at the *puertito* makes a very attractive walk, with plentiful bird-watching opportunities. The gorge is seen at its best when the sun is high enough to light up the interior — well before 4pm in the winter.

Start out by walking back up the **Puerto de los Molinos** access road (FV221; ○), with the **Barranco de los Molinos** on your left. It's a protected bird sanctuary visited at the end of the walk. Just past the first bend in the road, turn right on a wide track (**8min**), passing a large STONE GOATS' PEN.

The Barranco de los Molinos near the hide; although there is not much water in the barranco *here, down by its outlet to the sea it is likely to be running.*

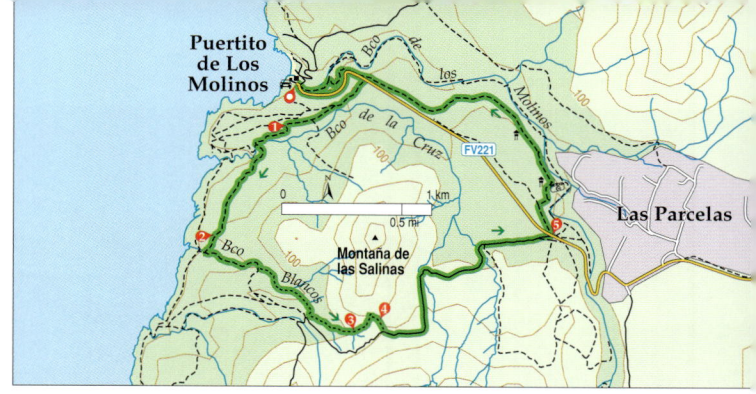

At a CAIRN (❶; **15min**), turn left on an eroded track down into the **Barranco de la Cruz**, but then climb out on the left after just 50m. A barren landscape lies ahead, bare of vegetation, while the ocean is in sight all the time.

Cross another small gully, and at another CAIRN you reach **Barranco Blancos** (❷; **35min**). Now a beautiful, wild coastline lies ahead of you. Take care scrambling down the eroded track into this *barranco!* Opposite are a rough STONE SHELTER and some interesting FOSSILIZED SAND FORMATIONS. Turn left along the dry riverbed, probably in the company of goats. After some 10 minutes, ignore a faint track off to the right. Keep to the river bed which narrows considerably about five minutes later (notice the interesting BEDROCK FORMATIONS here). When the BARRANCO SPLITS (❸; **1h05min**) keep left. After another five minutes, where the gully more or less ends, first go

The first restaurant and ducks at Puertito de los Molinos; just inland is the bridge shown below

left, then zigzag sharply up to the right, to a SADDLE (**4**; **1h10min**).

Las Parcelas, a pretty village of white houses, lies ahead of you. Take the track on your right and follow it to the left, passing another OLD STONE SHELTER. The track dips and winds its way through the landscape until it comes back to the FV221 (**5**; **1h45min**) near a car parking area. Cross the road at a sign about the protected bird sanctuary in the next *barranco*. A STONE-LINED TRAIL now leads you back into the **Barranco de los Molinos**, first past a viewpoint and then an OBSERVATION HIDE with an INFO PANEL ABOUT BIRDS and a bench (shaded from the setting sun in the afternoon). Water dripping from the *barranco* walls forms green 'curtains'. There are even some pools with water. Birds of all feathers fly in and out — it's a wonderful spot for bird-watchers (as is the reservoir visited in Walk 11 that feeds this *barranco*).

The stone-lined trail almost touches the road and then dips into the *barranco* once more just before coming back to **Puertito de los Molinos** and your starting point (**1**; **2h25min**).

Walk 11: EMBALSE DE LOS MOLINOS

Distance: 12.3km/7.6mi; 3h20min
Grade: 🔴 moderate; at times pathless, where you will need a good sense of direction, and over stony terrain. It can be very hot, and there is *no shade*. Ascent/descent of 300m/1000ft overall. The first part of the walk follows the GR 131 along a road

Equipment: walking boots or stout shoes with ankle support, walking poles, fleece, sunhat, suncream, raingear, picnic, plenty of water
Transport: 🚗 to/from Llanos de la Concepción; park at Bar García (28° 28.402'N, 14° 1.958'W); or 🚐 to/from Bar García (Line 02)

The Embalse de los Molinos is the largest reservoir on Fuerteventura. Its water level varies from year to year. For several years it was full to overflowing; as we go to press with this edition, it is only about half full. But it is still bursting with bird life — as is the Barranco de los Molinos, into which this reservoir empties. You can hope to see coots, egrets, herons, black-winged stilts, kestrels, and ruddy-shell ducks, as well as the ubiquitous gulls.

With your back to **Bar García** (⭕), turn left on the main FV30 and fork *half-left* immediately (*not* 90° left beside the bar). This road runs down into the village. For the first 40 minutes you'll head towards the rust-coloured conical hill ahead, then your way will swing left, before you ascend the hills over to your left to return to the bar/café. **Llanos de la Concepción**, a scattering of comfortable houses, is deep in slumber. Clumps of prickly-pear, a few thick-leafed aloes, and a variety of cacti sit behind the walls. Much of what was once cultivated now lies fallow. A road joins from the left, and you pass through an INTERSECTION where you join the **GR 131**. Two minutes later (170m further on), when the road forks, keep straight ahead, now on a track. Another track joins from the left a few minutes later, then a road after another minute. Follow this road down into a gully, where you cross a stream bed.

You head across a vast valley, its left side lined by smooth worn hills and its right side bordered by *cuchillos* (Spanish for 'knives': these are younger and sharper hills). The terrain is stony and dry. Solitary cultivated corners make a sharp contrast in this ochre-coloured landscape, with their vivid greenery. In spring scarlet poppies and daisies run amok in the gardens, and the plain is smeared with cereal-like *Gramineae*. You pass straight through another INTERSECTION (**20min**) and later ignore some turn-offs to the left. There is a development of modern houses in this area, with natural sandstone walls.

Approaching the **40min**-mark you again enter the STREAM BED (**❶**), just as it joins another coming from the right. A faint track goes left here. Under 100m from the confluence, you leave the stream bed and the main track as well, ascending a TRACK TO THE LEFT (**❷**). You immediately pass a small farm building on the left (ignore the track entering the gully on the right here). A large modern farmstead lies up ahead —

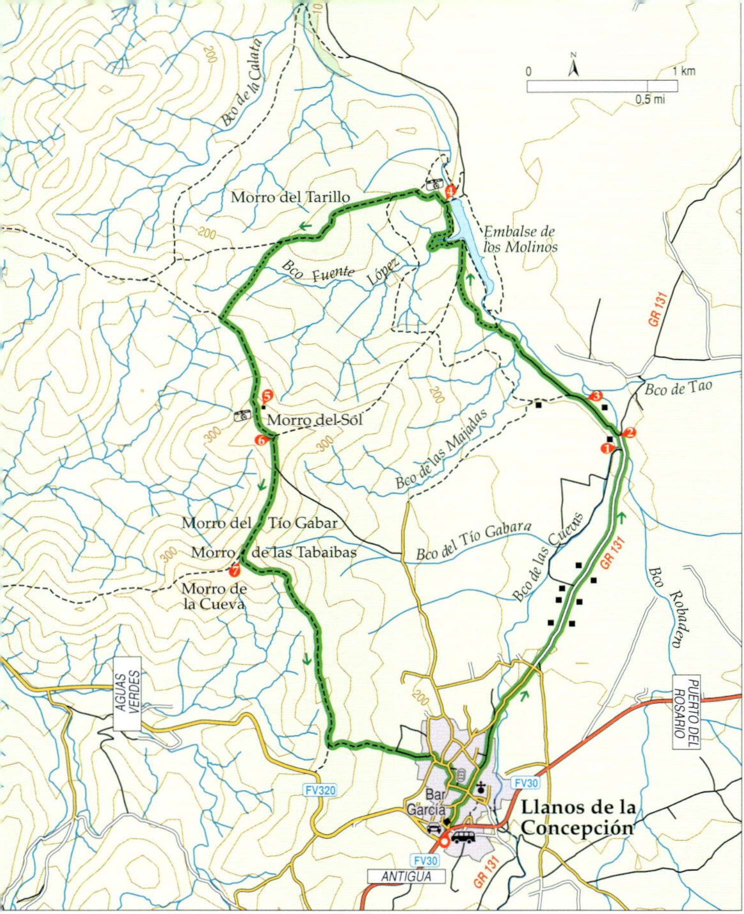

By the dam wall at the Embalse de los Molinos on a cloudy winter's day

Above: sharing the ridge above Llanos de la Concepción with some goats. The 'Great Wall' can be seen in the background, the fencing in the foreground. Right: cosco *is a feature on several corners of this walk.*

emitting a horrendous smell! Ignore a few minor tracks going off left and right. Soon a FIRST FENCE (❸) blocks your way. Go through the gate (please close it afterwards), or clamber over it. When the way swings up left to an old, abandoned farmhouse, keep straight ahead, following the *barranco* and crossing through a dense colony of ice plants and *cosco*.

You catch sight of the dam wall up ahead and gradually the tail of water below grows into a fully-fledged reservoir. If you're into ornithology, go quietly; birds do congregate around the muddy end of the dam here: once I saw dozens of coots. Continuing round the **Embalse de los Molinos**, you'll need to scramble up the rocky slopes and make your way around the inclines above it — one of the most attractive spots on the walk, where asphodels cover the slopes.

Around half an hour from the last fence you encounter a SECOND FENCE (**1h15min**). Follow it down to the edge of the reservoir. Now, if the water level is high, you won't be able to skirt it ... without disappearing into the mud! In which case you'll have to follow the fence up onto the headland for a few minutes, to where you can climb over it (there are stones on either side of the fence to help you). If the water level is not too high, make your way around the bottom of the fence, *first testing how soft the mud is!*

Once you've rounded the fence, an arm of water in a small side-*barranco* needs skirting. This is also a good spot for bird-watching, and you may see some herons. Keep around the edge of the arm of water and then ascend the side of the ridge. *Again, check any mud you intend to cross before ploughing straight on!*

Descending to the dam wall needs careful footwork; the hillside is steep and gravelly. If you're into bird-watching, you may like to cross the wall to a telescope on the eastern side. There's also a hide on the eastern side, but it's often locked.

From the DAM WALL (**4**; **1h30min**) scramble up onto the top of the crest above the dam, from where you'll have a good view over the reservoir and across the valley to the impressive barrier of hills. A small village of white houses (Las Parcelas, north of Walk 10) lies near the end of the valley. Red *cosco* stains the surrounding inclines, and a hint of green lies in the sheltered folds. The serenity and isolation of this landscape has a beauty all its own.

Home is now over the hills you've just circled. With your back to the *barranco* just below the dam (it's the **Barranco de los Molinos**, visited in Walk 10), head for the nearest round-topped hill. You follow a faint track that heads slightly left but then veers right near the top. From here, head for the highest peak visible: you may be able to see a wall descending from the top (from this angle it may look more like a dyke), and there is a ruined stone shelter part way up that you will pass on the ascent. Leaving the faint track, descend the rough ground to the left and, about 30 minutes from the dam wall, you cross the STREAM BED that runs between the two ridges (**2h**).

Now aim for the shoulder to the right of the peak. When you reach it you come onto a faint two-wheeled track and look straight out over another valley. Continue up the track to the left. Near the top of the crest you pass the STONE SHELTER (**5**) seen previously, just below, to your left, and soon the coast comes into view on your right. Close on **2h30min** you reach the second hilltop, **Morro del Sol**, the highest point in the walk (**6**; 351m/1150ft). Hold on to your hat! It's near the 'Great Wall' of Llanos de la Concepción (an impressive stretch of wall along the top of the ridge). Inland lie bare desiccated hills, climbing one upon the other.

Remaining on the track, pass through the wall and follow it along the top of the ridge, to the right. Two minutes along you pass through the goat fencing once more (the wire-mesh gate may be hard to see at first; make sure it is securely fastened behind you). Llanos de la Concepción is now in sight below. Valle de Santa Inés huddles high in the hills ahead. Ignore a track going off the mountain here. Close on 15 minutes beyond the wall, your track swings up left onto a lateral ridge heading towards Llanos de la Concepción (**Morro de las Tabaibas; 7**), while the wall and the fence continue to the right. More of Santa Inés opens up — and terracing, stepping shallow *barrancos*.

Some 20 minutes downhill, with a road not far ahead, leave the track and descend left to the village on a fainter track (where there may be a goat enclosure). Walk cross-country for some 70m/yds, to a clear track lined by a stone wall. When you hit asphalt, use the map to make your way past the school and back to **Bar García** (**O**; **3h20min**).

Walk 12: FROM ANTIGUA TO BETANCURIA

Distance: 5.5km/3.5mi; 1h50min
Grade: 🔴 fairly strenuous, with an ascent of 340m/1120ft, much of it up a stony path; well waymarked (SL FV 29 and partly GR 131)
Equipment: walking boots, sunhat, light jacket, suncream, picnic, plenty of water; raingear in winter

Transport: 🚐 to Antigua (Line 01); return on 🚐 from Betancuria (Line 02). If travelling by car, you could park in Antigua and take the 16.30 🚐 from Vega de Río Palmas via Betancuria to Puerto del Rosario and change to a Line 01 bus back to Antigua (ask the driver where to set you down) — but it would be easier to just call a taxi (✆ 928 163004).

Betancuria, with the 17th-century cathedral church of Santa Maria

78 Landscapes of Fuerteventura

This is the pilgrim's walk. Every year on the third Saturday in September hundreds of pilgrims make their way across these hills to pay homage to the Virgen de la Peña in Vega de Río Palmas. The contrast you'll see in vegetation is reason enough to do the hike. In winter there's a rare lushness on the hilltops rarely seen on this island, and grass abounds.

The walk begins at the CHURCH in **Antigua** (⬤). With the belfry behind you and the leafy square on your left, head along the street to the first junction. Turn right here (there is a fingerpost for the 'DEGOLLADA DEL MARRUBIO' and 'BETANCURIA'). Go through another junction and soon cross the valley floor. Palms border the

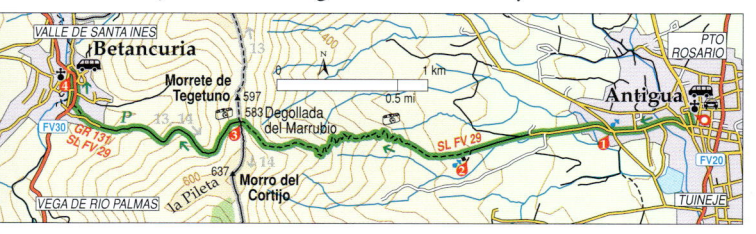

Walk 12: From Antigua to Betancuria 79

road. Ignore two roads to the left and, shortly after, a road to the right. Within **10min** you'll see a WATER TANK (❶) on the right, and a Y-FORK ahead. Take the fork to the left, which goes straight ahead towards the barrier of hills cutting across in front of you. You can see your ongoing route from this point — a wide path ascending a lateral crest not far ahead, offset slightly to the right.

Around 10 minutes later ignore a road to the left. Some 90m/yds further on, when the road forks right, continue straight ahead on a track (FINGERPOST). Most of the garden plots on the left lie fallow. Just below a WATERHOUSE (❷), the way forks. Head right up the wide **SL FV 29** path, the ascent now noticeable. A lush little cultivated valley unravels to your left and, looking back down over the scattering of Antigua, you have a sweeping view. Low volcanic humps and razor-backed ridges stretch across the horizon.

A SIGN designating the area *'parque rural'* comes up just over **30min** en route. You zigzag your way uphill towards the crest. Nearer the top, the spiny *aulaga* bushes give way to bright green *tabaiba*. The path fades briefly, but traces of stone walls come to the rescue. In winter low cloud may brush the ridges. The terrain gets rockier, and the greens of the *verode*, *tabaiba* and asphodelus bring life to these otherwise insipid slopes. Then the grass becomes noticeable; the landscape softens. Quite a treat! Soon goats and sheep will keep you company.

Crossing the **Degollada del Marrubio** (or Degollada de la Villa; ❸; **1h20min**), brace yourself for a blasting on windy days! A brilliant sight awaits you now, as the vegetation changes completely. The inclines are dotted with wind-battered pines, and grass carpets the ground. Straight below lies Betancuria, ensconced in these hills. Keeping straight over the crest, past the shelter, you descend on a very wide path. Thick leathery-leafed aloes border the path and nearby fields. Baying dogs welcome you into **Betancuria** 25 minutes below the pass, and you turn right on reaching the FV30. The bus stops about 200m/yds beyond the Valtarajal Restaurant, just before the BRIDGE (❹; **1h50min**).

The walk beings with Antigua's leafy church square on your left.

Walk 13: MIRADOR DE MORRO VELOSA

See map overleaf; see also photos overleaf and on page 77
Distance: 6km/3.7mi; 2h15min
Grade: 🔴 moderate, with an overall ascent/descent of 365m/1200ft on mostly wide paths and tracks; well signposted and white/green/red waymarked GR 131 and SL FV 29
Equipment: walking boots, walking pole(s), sunhat, light jacket, suncream, picnic, plenty of water; raingear in winter
Transport: 🚗 to Betancuria (several large car parks; the nearest is at 28° 25.523'N, 14° 3.414'W); or 🚐 to/from Betancuria (Line 02)

Short walk: Convento de San Buenaventura (1km; 20min). 🔵 A straightforward stroll on roads and a pretty path. Transport as main walk; only stout shoes needed. With your back to the bus shelter below the church at Betancuria, turn left; then take the first right — a level road. Ignore the sign for the SL FV 10 and a track ahead; bend right on asphalt, then go left at a T-junction. After just 120m on this rising road, turn left on a path beside the *barranco* (sign: *CONVENTO*) to the ruined **Convento de San Buenaventura** (❺) and return the same way.

After a stiff climb, the roller-coaster walk along the tops affords really splendid views over a large part of the island. Enjoy them now! Because your goal is the best-known viewpoint on Fuerteventura, where you will meet convoys of orange tour coaches disgorging hoards of day-trippers. Queue for some refreshment at the café if you can stand the crowds, before you begin your rather gravelly decent back to Betancuria. On the way back you will come to *my* favourite part of this walk — the utterly peaceful, beautiful ruined convent of San Buenaventura.

Start at the BUS SHELTER (⬤) below the CHURCH at **Betancuria**: follow Walk 14 on page 71 up to the **Degollada del Marrubio** (❶; 40min), with its two picnic tables in a small shelter. From this pass the GR 131 continues to the right (to Vega de Río Palmas; Walk 14), but for this hike keep left, still ascending between Antigua's plain to the east and Betancuria's valley to the west. The path follows a

Looking north from the Mirador de Morro Velosa

Walk 13: Mirador de Morro Velosa

STONE WALL up to the summit of **Tegú** (②; **1h**), from where the Jandía massif is visible.

On the descent from Tegú the trail bends to the eastern side of the ridge, running through a gap in the STONE WALL (③; **1h15min**). You arrive on another saddle, the **Degollada de Maninubre**, then climb again — to a WATERHOUSE. We will return to this point to finish the walk but, for now, continue on the track, then head up to the **Mirador de Morro Velosa**, closed at present for rebuilding (④; **1h25min**). When it reopens, it should have a bar/café and museum. On a clear day El Cotillo is visible in the northwest, with Lanzarote beyond. On a *very* clear day Gran Canaria and Teide on Tenerife are visible.

From the mirador go back to the WATERHOUSE and descend the badly eroded, rather steep and skiddy track on the right, going down into the valley called **Majada de la Perra**, where Betancuria's church is visible at the bottom. At the bottom of the valley there is a series of earthen dams (*presas secas;* see page 18) to gather water in the rainy season. Cane, tamarisk and agave grow in the dry valley floor, then palms announce your arrival in the old town of Betancuria.

The trail merges with a crossing track that takes you to the right, and you pass above the ruined **Convento de San Buenaventura** (⑤). From here follow the tarred road back to **Betancuria** (O; **2h15min**), but perhaps first visit the convent shown overleaf.

The Short walk follows this pretty path in the Barranco del Convento to the ruined convent of San Buenaventura — perhaps my favourite part of this walk. As the main walk heads down the road from above the convent, turn sharp right just before a bridge and follow the barranco to the lovely building.

Walk 14: FROM BETANCURIA TO VEGA DE RIO PALMAS

See map opposite and photos on pages 20-21 and 77
Distance: 7.1km/4.4mi; 2h40min
Grade: 🔴 moderate, with an ascent of 255m/836ft and descent of 370m/ 1210ft, on good tracks and paths. This is the GR 131, well signposted and waymarked (red/white) throughout.
Equipment: walking boots, walking pole(s), sunhat, light jacket, suncream, picnic, plenty of water; raingear in winter
Transport: 🚗 to Betancuria (several large car parks; the nearest is at 28° 25.523'N, 14° 3.414'W); or 🚌 to Betancuria (Line 02). Return on 🚌 from Vega de Río Palmas (Line 02 — back to base, or back to Betancuria to pick up your car.
Short walk: Degollada del Marrubio (3.5km/2.2mi; 1h20min). 🔵 Straightforward ascent/descent of 200m/650ft on a wide, signposted and waymarked path — a good, if demanding, leg-stretcher on a car tour. Equipment and transport as main walk. Follow the main walk to the **Degollada del Marrubio** (**❶**) and return the same way.

I make no excuse for describing so many walks around Betancuria and Vega de Río Palmas. There is some verdure — relief from the miles of bland and barren, dusty tracks. This walk is a good example: it leads through the island's only pine 'wood' — tiny, but a most welcome splash of greenery.

Start at the BUS SHELTER (**○**) below the CHURCH at **Betancuria**: walk south on the FV30 towards Vega de Río Palmas. Just 50m past the bar-restaurant VALTARAJAL, turn left on a crazy-paved walkway with a white/green/red waymark. Head straight uphill. The trail climbs to a road (CALLE BUENAVENTURA). Follow this uphill for 100m; then, where the tarmac swings left, keep straight ahead on an earthen track at the left of the fingerpost shown on page 37, to rise up the **GR 131/ SL FV 29**. Your track is lined with agaves and in the *barranco* on the left you may spot a buzzard or two. Eventually you reach a saddle, the **Degollada del Marrubio** (**❶**; **40min**), with two picnic tables in a small shelter and wonderful views in all directions.

Turn right uphill here and follow the **GR 131** along the ridge up to **Morro del Cortijo** (**❷**; **1h05min**) from where you can see both the west and east coasts … and down to your goal — Vega de Río Palmas. From this high point follow a fence (crossing it twice) down to a saddle below the transmitters on Morro Janana, the **Degollada de los Pasos** (**❸**; **1h20min**). Follow the GR to the right here through a wooden gate.

Now a wide track takes over, leading through the island's only — minuscule — PINE WOOD. The trees are small and wind-weary, but in a few places you'll have the excitement of spotting *moss* hanging from the branches! You look out to the highest peak in the central massif, Pico de Betancuria. Ten minutes down from the pass you come to the **Castillo de Lara** picnic area (**❹**; **1h30min**) — full to bursting on weekends.

Just above the picnic area the GR continues along the left side of the valley on a log-stepped path. You're likely to be accompanied by

Top: looking down on the Aula de Naturaleza Parra Medina; below: at the Casa de los Padrones, with a view to the antennae on Morro Janana

buzzards and crows. Soon you have another view of the Vega de Río Palmas valley from a ruined house. A few minutes later you come to the **Casa de los Padrones** (**5**; **1h45min**), recently restored by the island government. This 12-bed refuge works together with the **Aula de Naturaleza Parra Medina** a short way downhill to offer environmental education.

Meeting a track at the *Aula*, follow it downhill for a good 10 minutes. Then, shortly before the FV30, take a stepped path down into the dry bed of the **Río Palmas** and go under the road via an UNDERPASS (**6**; **2h10min**). Follow the river bed for 10 minutes more, at which point it bends left at the confluence with another dry gully. Continue for a good 20 minutes, then climb out to the CHURCH SQUARE and BUS STOP in **Vega de Río Palmas** (**7**; **2h40min**). Have a coffee on the charming patio of the restaurant Don Antonio next to the church (closed Wednesdays), while you wait for your bus.

Walk 15: FROM TISCAMANITA TO VEGA DE RIO PALMAS

See also photos on pages 20-21 and opposite
Distance: 9.2km/5.7mi; 3h40min (including detour to Gran Montaña)
Grade: 🔴 fairly strenuous, with an ascent of 515m/1690ft (almost all in one go) and a descent of 470m/1540ft (some of it on gravelly paths). All paths are clear, well-waymarked and signed (green/white SL FV 31) except for the detour to Gran Montaña which is almost pathless
Equipment: walking boots, walking pole(s), sunhat, light jacket, suncream, picnic, plenty of water; raingear in winter
Transport: 🚐 to Tiscamanita (Line 01); return on 🚐 from Vega de Río Palmas (Line 02). 🚗 Driving is not recommended: it does not make sense to park at either end of the walk (unless you have two cars); the distance by road is too great for reasonable taxi fares. But you might leave a car at Casillas del Angel, which is on the route of both bus Lines 01 and 02.

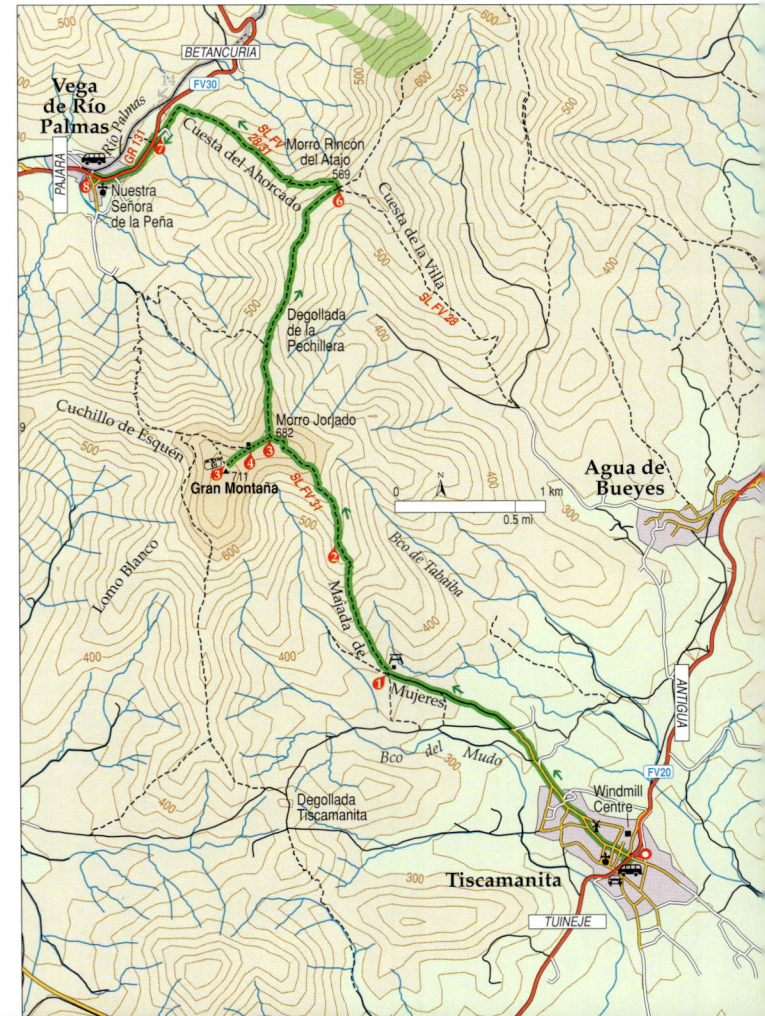

86   Landscapes of Fuerteventura

If you have the energy for the initial climb, this is a beautiful walk with far-reaching views in all directions. The old trail between Tiscamanita and Vega de Río Palmas has recently been restored by the island government to make a fine 'local' walk, the SL FV 31.

Start out on the main road in **Tiscamanita**: 50m northeast of the bus shelter, watch for the brown road sign *'CENTRO DE INTERPRETACION DE LOS MOLINOS'* and turn west on CALLE JUAN PEÑATE (**⊙**). Ten metres along is a hikers' INFORMATION BOARD on the left. Continue into the village, ignoring all side-streets and tracks; stay on JUAN PEÑATE. After passing a derelict OLD ALOE FARM on the right, the way becomes a signposted dirt track, and you climb past some traditional wind-pumps and *gavias* (see page 41) over to the left. An INFORMATION BOARD explains the different types of agriculture in this area; you will pass many examples.

Left: from the trig point on the top of Gran Montaña the entire south of the island opens up; below: you pass this derelict aloe farm just at the start of the walk. Tiscamanita is an open-air museum of traditional island agriculture.

Walk 15: From Tiscamanita to Vega de Río Palmas

When you reach a SHELTER with two picnic tables and a SIGNPOST (❶; **35min**) climb the stone-lined path at the left of the shelter, accompanied by ravens and goats. You pass fields of *tuneras* (*Opuntia* cacti used in the past for cochineal production) and *pitas* (agaves yielding sisal and rope). There are also *cuernúas* (*Caralluma burchardii*, a small and endangered plant endemic to the eastern Canaries), *acebuche majorero* (*Olea europea ssp guarchicha,* an olive tree species), *tabaibas* and *verode*.

The higher you climb along the **Majada de Mujeres** (a protected area, where shepherds kept their flocks at night), the better the view. Eventually, you can see to Montaña Cardón (Walk 23) in the south, the Jandía Massif (Walks 24-27), and the Chilea mountain range behind Pájara. To the north are views over Antigua and the central mountains, settings for Walks 12-14 — and the walk you are on.

You reach an elongated SADDLE above the Majada de Mujeres (❷; **1h10min**). Continue to another saddle, **Morro Jorjado** (❸; **1h40min**) which harbours, as the name suggests, colonies of *jorjado* (*Asteriscus sericeus*). From here head up steeply left on a barely visible but signposted path. You pass a ruined OLD SHELTER (❹), and after 15 minutes you're on the summit of **Gran Montaña** (❺; **1h55min**), the viewpoint shown opposite.

Now it takes another 15 minutes to slide back down to **Morro Jorjado** and continue north on the path, via the **Degollada de la Pechillera**. Five minutes down this trail you pass another OLD SHELTER, and in the next 20 minutes you will pass three more — all barely more than a low, rounded stone wall to protect shepherds from the elements.

After reaching a small peak, fencing starts on your left. A few minutes later you come to the **Morro del Rincón del Atajo** (❻; **2h55min**), where you join another local walk coming from Água de Bueyes; it's the **SL FV 28**, although no sign tells you so. Go through a gate on the left here and head down the trail, passing another RUINED SHELTER after five minutes.

Descend the **Cuesta del Ahorcado** until you reach the **FV30** (❼; **3h30min**). Follow the road to the left now, to the CHURCH and the Plaza de Nuestra Señora de la Peña in **Vega de Río Palmas** (❽; **3h40min**), shown on pages 21-21. The restaurant Don Antonio, next to the church (closed Wednesdays), has a lovely patio, where you could wait for your bus with some refreshment.

Walk 16: BARRANCO DE LAS PEÑITAS

See also photos on pages 13, 17, 20-21, 24, 41, 91
Distance: 4.4km/2.7mi; 1h40min
Grade: 🔵❗ quite easy, well signposted and waymarked (SL FV 06/27), but the path to the chapel could prove unnerving for those prone to vertigo. *Be very careful if it's wet!* The extension to the Arco de las Peñitas (**ⓑ**), almost pathless, is *very steep* (●), but not vertiginous if you approach from the east. **Not for everyone!**
Equipment: comfortable shoes or walking boots, fleece, sunhat, suncream, raingear, picnic, water
Transport: 🚗 to/from Vega de Río Palmas. From the church drive south on the FV30 and turn right after just under 400m on the narrow road to the reservoir (signposted to Vega de Río Palmas); park by a bridge at the signposted entrance to the path/track into the stream bed (28° 23.617N, 14° 5.266'W). Or 🚐 to/from Vega de Río Palmas (Line 02); alight at the 'Casa de la Naturaleza' bus shelter (**ⓐ**) and walk downhill 150m to the bridge where the signposted walk begins.
Short walk: Nuestra Señora de la Peña (2.4km/1.5mi; 30min). Grade/equipment as above. *Not signposted*. Transport by 🚗: take the FV605 from Pájara towards La Pared and turn right after 1.5km on the FV621. Turn right again after 3km on a road signposted to Buen Paso (FV627). After 1.2km the road is chained off: either park here (**ⓒ** ; 28° 23.165N, 14° 6.682'W) and walk along the track into the **Barranco de Mal Paso**, or drive to where you can see the chapel in its narrow gorge. Cross the *barranco* bed at this point and follow a walled-in water pipe to a RUIN, from where a pretty path leads to **Nuestra Señora de la Peña** (**②**).

Walk 16: Barranco de las Peñitas

This stroll is short and sweet; it takes you down one of the island's most picturesque valleys, the Barranco de las Peñitas. Palm trees dot the valley, and a small reservoir (sadly dry recently) rests in the floor. From the reservoir wall you look through a corridor of rock out onto more palms and salubrious garden plots far below. In winter you may find dark green pools embedded in the floor of the *barranco*. Hidden in the sheer walls lies the delightful little Ermita de Nuestra Señora de la Peña — just the kind of place where one might feel inclined to offer up a prayer.

Start the walk in **Vega de Río Palmas** at the BRIDGE over the **Barranco de las Peñitas** (○): take the gravel track that strikes off right just before the stream bed and drops down into the dry stream bed (**SL FV 06/27**). A healthy sprinkling of tall palms graces the valley floor and the entire valley. For Fuerteventura, this is the height of arboreal luxury! Abrupt craggy ridges dominate the landscape. Follow the stream bed until, a little over **10min** off the road, the ways climbs up right out of the *barranco* on a wide old washed-out track. When the track forks, go left to skirt the reservoir on the trail. A sign indicates that this area is a bird sanctuary.

The valley floor quickly fills with tamarisk and then forks. The left-hand fork swings back up into the hills; the right-hand fork cradles the reservoir, before folding up into a narrow ravine that drops down to join the Barranco de Mal Paso. You're surrounded by hills, with the pointed Gran Montaña (708m/2320ft; Walk 15) dominating the valley. The now-narrow trail winds amidst large boulders. Soon the **Presa de las Peñitas** is just below you. It used to be half-full of murky green water at least in winter and spring. Now it has been bone dry for a few years whatever the season. But green garden plots set amidst palm trees terrace the slopes on your left. The *barranco* is freckled with verode — the brightest plant on the slopes. Less than 10 minutes along, you're on the RESERVOIR WALL (❶; **30min**). The ravine closes up into a deep V, before emptying out onto an oasis of palms and gardens and continuing its seaward journey.

Nuestra Señora de la Peña sits above the palm-choked Barranco de Mal Paso

Beyond the reservoir wall you follow a stone-paved path built into the sides of the *barranco*. Parts have crumbled away, requiring steady footwork ... and the lizards darting about are distracting. The pools may be just puddles by the time you visit, but they *can* be very deep. A couple of minutes down the path, you spot the tiny white chapel of **Nuestra Señora de la Peña** (❷), perched on a rocky outcrop above the stream bed. A short stretch of path leads to it. This path clings to the face of the rock and is quite unnerving, but it's fairly short — only some 30m/yds.

Inside the chapel you'll find bits of clothing, plastic flowers, and a visitors' book that makes for interesting reading. Beyond the *ermita* sometimes the path hangs out over the side of the *barranco* — unnerving for those without a head for heights. It's an impressive piece of path-building, that's for sure. A few minutes along, you pass a RUIN (❸; **50min**) and can see the course of the Short walk from Buen Paso. Some 35m/yds past the ruin, decide whether you are going to tackle the climb to the Arco de las Peñitas. A few minutes later the path makes a U-turn to the south, a good viewpoint. There is another path to the Arco here,

The Arco de las Peñitas

but if you take it, keep heading right to approach from the east.

Returning, follow the same route, remaining on the path just above the reservoir until you re-enter the stream bed. You should be back at the BRIDGE (❶) in **Vega de Río Palmas** in **1h40min**. The BUS SHELTER is just 150m up the road, in front of the CASA DE LA NATURALEZA.

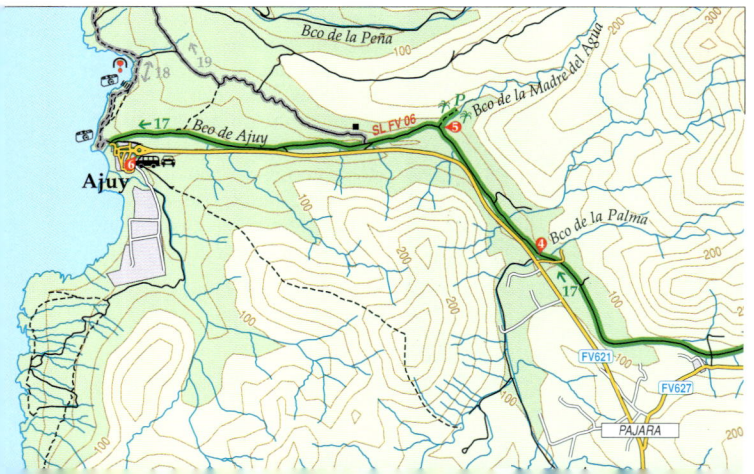

Walk 17: FROM VEGA DE RIO PALMAS TO AJUY

See also photos on pages 20-21, 24, 41, 88-89, 92, 94-95
Distance: 8.7km/5.4mi; 2h30min
Grade: 🔵 ❗ quite easy, with an overall descent of 250m/820ft. Well signposted and waymarked (SL FV 06), but the path to the chapel could prove unnerving for those prone to vertigo. *Be very careful if it's wet!*
Equipment: stout shoes (walking boots preferable), fleece, sunhat, suncream, raingear, picnic, plenty of water

Transport: 🚗 or 🚐 to Vega de Río Palmas as Walk 16, page 88. There is no convenient bus for the return, so the best solution is to pre-book a (fairly expensive) taxi from Pájara to collect you at Ajuy and take you back to your car at Vega de Río Palmas (📞 928 547032 (Costa Calma taxi) or 📞 928 541257 (Morro Jable taxi). Otherwise see Walk 19 on page 94: park in Ajuy and walk *up* the *barranco*.

If you're out for the day in this area and itching to put on the boots, no doubt you'll find Walk 16 too short. This extension is very satisfying. The only problem is getting back to your car, unless you are walking with friends and have two cars or enough people to make the taxi cost economical.

Start out by following Walk 16 on page 88 to the RUIN (❸; **50min**). Take the path just above the RUIN that curves round and left, down into the floor of the **Barranco de las Peñitas** and then the **Barranco de Mal Paso** cutting down in front of you. Ignore all farm tracks left and right.

You cross a road in the **Barranco de la Palma** (❹; **1h30min**) and about 20 minutes later spot a small valley chock full of palms cutting back into the hillside on your right. After the *ermita* and the pools in the Peñitas Gorge, this is the second highlight of the walk: the **Barranco de la Madre del Água** (❺; **1h50min**), shown on pages 94-95). *Do* go and investigate this shady oasis — a beautiful spot.

Then return to the main *barranco* (now the **Barranco de Ajuy**) and continue down to **Ajuy** (❻; **2h30min**). Time to tack on Walk 18 before you call it a day?

The Presa de las Peñitas before it dried up, but tamarisk trees still grace its tail.

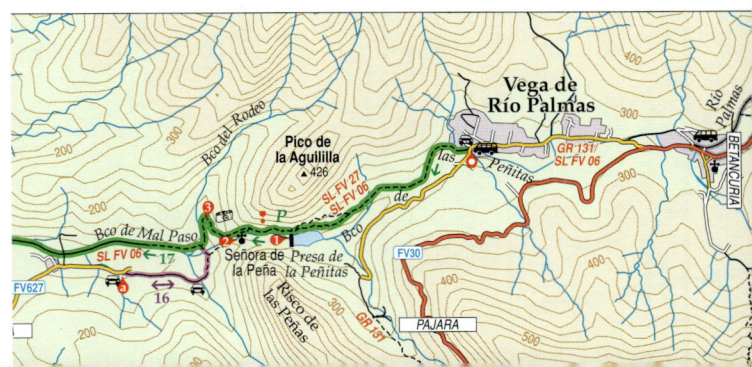

Walk 18: AJUY'S SEA CAVES AND PLAYA DEL JURADO

See also photos on pages 96-97
Distance: 3.7km/2.3mi; 1h30min
Grade: ● easy, but with ankle-twisting terrain underfoot. *Don't* venture too close to the edge of the cliffs — they could crumble away easily, *and take care on the steps down to the caves!*
Equipment: shoes with good ankle support, fleece, sunhat, raingear, suncream, swimwear, picnic, water
Transport: 🚗 to/from Ajuy. Park at the turning circle at the entrance to the village (28° 23.970'N, 14° 9.267'W), or down by the beach. (Line 04 🚐 serves Ajuy from Pájara, but timings are not convenient, unless you want to spend the entire day.)

You'll be awed by the striking coastal scenery on this walk, which leads past a mirador above two enormous sea caves at Caleta Negra and then to Peña Horadada, an impressive rock pierced with a hole. But now there's more! In June 2017 news was released that the sea caves may well have harboured German U-boats during WWII — under the

Walk 18: Ajuy's sea caves and Playa del Jurado 93

protection of the (in)famous Herr Gustav Winter at Cofete. You can read all about it at warhistoryfans.com or just key in 'Ajuy caves' and 'Winter' for the latest news articles (including some from the BBC).

Start the walk at the TURNING CIRCLE at the entrance to **Ajuy** (**O**): descend into the village of dazzling white houses until you reach the black sandy beach stretching out to the left. Now you follow the crowds to ascend a beautiful stone-laid path past an INFORMATION BOARD about the geology of this area (perhaps the most interesting in all the Canaries). The black-sand beach and the cluster of little white houses make a striking contrast. Rounding the rock wall of the *barranco*, you come upon a spectacular view: from chalk-white rock terraces (a fossilized beach, just one of the rare geological features!) you look across a blue sea towards cliffs hollowed out by massive caves. You'll pass every tourist and his dog on this path — the short stretch up to the Caleta Negra *mirador* is in every brochure. When the path forks, take the upper branch; the lower one descends to a coastal platform.

A little over **10min** will bring you to the *mirador* (**❶**) above **Caleta Negra** — a viewing balcony in the face of the cliff. The paved steps down to it are protected by sturdy wooden railings, as are those down to the TWO ENORMOUS CAVES mentioned above (one of them is shown on pages 96-97). Further steps continue down to the sea, but these are narrow, vertiginous and unprotected — take care, especially if it's wet or the sea's rough.

To continue on to Playa del Jurado, head back up the path and veer sharply up to the left, to the clifftops above. Now you've left the crowds behind. A path, partly marked with cairns, takes you along the cliffs and round the shoreline. After crossing a gully, from this side of the bay you can look back towards the *mirador,* to see more caves carved into the cliffs. It's a spectacular piece of coastline.

Head straight across this slightly raised flat area. Soon you'll see the jagged tail of a *barranco* wall ahead. Aim straight for it. Playa del Jurado comes into sight — with a monument of rock, Fuerteventura's own 'Arc de Triomphe', perched at the water's edge. The easiest place to descend to the beach is down the gentle slope just opposite the mouth of the **Barranco de la Peña** — straight down to **Peña Horadada** (also called **Arco del Jurado**; **❷**; **40min**). Otherwise take the clear track down to **Playa del Jurado** (**❸**) — where 'alternative lifestylers' camp from time to time. Tamarisk trees huddle along the valley floor. Unfortunately, cans and bottles are often scattered about here, so watch out for broken glass. And remember that *the beaches here are deadly dangerous!*

Return the way you came or follow the shoreline; timings are about the same, and you will be back at the TURNING CIRCLE in **Ajuy** (**O**) in **1h30min**.

Left: Ajuy and its beach, from the walkway to the caves and Playa del Jurado

Walk 19: FIVE-STAR CIRCUIT FROM AJUY

See also photo on page 92
Distance: 8.7km/5.4mi; 2h25min
Grade: ● easy, but on the return walk don't venture too close to the edge of the cliffs — they could easily crumble away, *and be prepared to take extra time on the narrow steps to the caves.*
Equipment: shoes with good ankle support (or walking boots), fleece, sunhat, raingear, suncream, swimwear, picnic, water
Refreshments: ample in Ajuy
Transport: 🚗 to/from Ajuy. Park as for Walk 18, page 92. No bus access.
Shorter walk: Barranco de la Madre del Água (5.3km/3.3mi; 1h25min). ● very easy. Follow the walk to the PALM GROVE shown below (❷); return the same way.

This walk makes the most of the varied landscapes in this little pocket of Fuerteventura *and* delves into some recent history linking Ajuy's caves with World War II. The first part of the walk leads into one of the island's most salubrious corners, where you'll fine a tiny stream that flows all year round; in the second half you'll be awed by the striking coastal scenery and perhaps as intrigued as we were to read about the history of the two enormous caves below the *mirador*.

Start out at the ROUNDABOUT (O) in **Ajuy**: head down to the beach (or park there and begin there). Then, rather than following everyone else straight to the cliffs, curl right and follow the track up the **Barranco de Ajuy**. Eventually you will notice another TRACK crossing the *barranco* (❶; **30-35min**) — note this for your return, but keep straight on. Some 500m further on, you come to a side valley on your left, crammed with palms — the **Barranco de la Madre del Água** (❷; **45min**). It's sheer bliss in the shade of trees here, listening to the trickle of water.

When you're ready to leave, retrace your steps for about seven minutes, to the TRACK (❶) crossed earlier. Follow this up to the right, past some RUINED HOUSES. *(But for the Shorter walk, keep straight ahead, retracing your outward route.)*

At the mouth of the Barranco de la Madre del Água — a tiny, permanently flowing stream and a profusion of palms

Walk 19: Five-star circuit from Ajuy

Ignore a track off to the right after just under 1km. Shortly after, go through a rickety FENCE. Then ignore another track to the right a little over 1km further on.

Coming into the **Barranco de la Peña**, turn left among tamarisk trees lining the valley floor. Well under an hour after leaving the palm oasis you are facing **Peña Horadada** (❸) at **Playa del Jurado** (❹; **1h35min**). Please

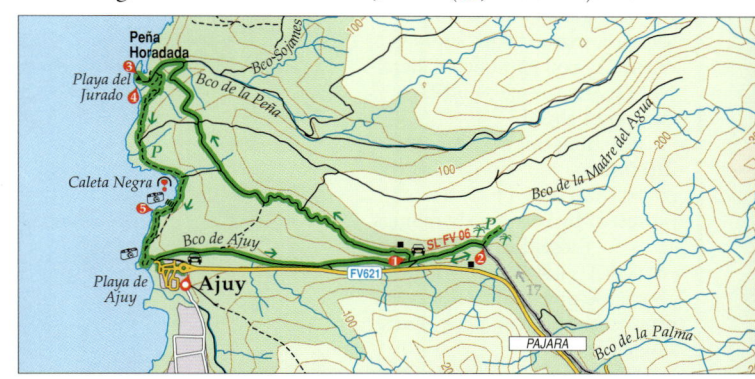

96 Landscapes of Fuerteventura

remember that beaches here on the island's west coast are *very dangerous!*

From the beach you can either climb straight up to the cliffs or take the gentler inland path. The way along the cliffs is straight-forward, marked with sporadic cairns. As you approach **Caleta Negra** you can see a cliff-face viewpoint ahead.

Reaching this *mirador* (**5**; **2h10min**), you will see that the paved steps down to it are protected by very sturdy railings — as are those down to the TWO ENORMOUS CAVES mentioned above. Be prepared to lose some time on the narrow steps — it's single file only!

These caves form part of the Betancuria Rural Park and are one

Right: one of the sea caves at Ajuy.
News broke in 2017 that these huge caves may have harboured German U-boats during the Second World War — under the direction of a certain Señor Winter. You can read about it by just keying in 'Ajuy sea caves' for news articles (including some from the BBC). At isolated Cofete, on the southern tip of the island (Walk 27), there's a large house surmounted by a turret. It was built by Señor Winter who forbade anyone else to live in the area. The house is now inhabited by the grandson of one of the builders, who has become a bit of a celebrity — running tours of the property. He even has a facebook page. But it's a sad story, which you can read on casawinter.com. There are also videos on YouTube, including tours of the house. Was the white-tiled 'kitchen' really an operating theatre performing plastic surgery on notorious Nazis before they fled to South America? Fascinating stuff.

Opposite: Peña Horadada, also called Arco del Jurado, at the mouth of the Barranco de la Peña. Right: the fossilized dune landscape at Caleta Negra, near the mirador, *is fascinating to look at, but quite tricky underfoot. Below: flights of narrow steps with sturdy railings lead down to a first sea-cave; it's certainly large enough to shelter a submarine (see the caption below left). If the sea is not too rough, you can make your way into the adjacent cave.*

of the world's 150 main sites of geological interest: they are the oldest rock formations in the Canary Islands, created by the flow of lava which rose 100 million years ago from a depth of 3000 metres beneath the sea.

From the viewpoint it's little more than 10 minutes back to **Ajuy** and your car (**2h25min**).

Walk 20: LAS SALINAS AND PUERTO DE LA TORRE

See also photo on page 43
Distance: 13.8km/8.6mi; 3h30min
Grade: ● easy, mostly along an almost-level promenade and then a gravel track, with a brief stretch along the clifftops. Short descent/ascent into and out of the Barranco de la Torre.
Equipment: comfortable walking shoes, light jacket, swimwear, sunhat, raingear, suncream, picnic, plenty of water. *Note:* the Restaurant Caracolitos, mentioned below, is closed Sundays (at time of writing).
Transport: 🚗 to/from Caleta de Fuste; park on the south side of the resort outside the Geranios Suites, just north of the large Sheraton (28° 23.601'N, 13° 51.666'W). Or 🚌 (Line 03); walk to the Geranios Suites to begin (1km/0.62 mi return)
Short walk: Las Salinas
(7km/4.3mi; 2h). ● Very easy; access/equipment as above. Follow the main walk to **Las Salinas** and retrace steps — or return by Line 03 🚌 (frequent), making the walk only 3.5km.
Longer walk: Pozo Negro
(18km/11mi; 5h). ● Moderate on account of the length; overall ups and downs of about 200m/650ft; transport and equipment as main walk. Follow the main walk to (**a**), then continue to **Pozo Negro** where Walk 21 begins. Follow the first part of Walk 21, but continue up to the main FV2 for 🚌 Line 10 back to base or back to Caleta de Fuste (two buses in the afternoon, Mon-Sat).

I have to admit that, for me, this walk doesn't rate as highly as the Restaurant Caracolitos en route. My mouth still waters when I think about the mussels done in garlic and a spicy local sauce that they served up. Ah, yes, the walk... The Short walk (the very popular stretch to the salt pans and the restaurant) makes a pleasant late afternoon stroll, especially if you have a late lunch or snack in mind! The best part of the hike, however, is *beyond* the restaurant, where you dip into a pretty little *barranco* filled with palms and verdant succulents. Then, out of the *barranco,* a magnificent stretch of coastline awaits you, and it's unlikely you'll have to share it with a soul … or even the ubiquitous goat.

Start out on the south side of **Caleta de Fuste**, at the GERANIOS SUITES. Follow the seaside promenade south past the array of hotels and shops catering for beach- and golf-lovers. When the promenade ends abruptly, head towards the shore and pick up a sandy track. Before long you come to a road into **Las Salinas del Carmen**, a huddle of white dwellings set on a slope overlooking a small beach. To the left is the MUSEO DE LA SAL (**1**; Salt Museum; **55min**), well worth a visit. Beyond it are the salt pans, backed by the much-photographed skeleton of a fin whale that expired near Corralejo. Now go and find *the* restaurant (LOS CARACOLITOS; **2**). It overlooks the sandy beach and it's tremendously friendly. *Buen provecho!*

Continuing out of Las Salinas — in company with the **SL FV 08** which runs south to Pozo Negro

Walk 20: Las Salinas and the Barranco del Torre 99

— follow the narrow road behind the village until it curves back to the sea and becomes a track. Over the crest you look down onto the small black-sand beach of Puerto de la Torre, with a couple of derelict buildings, tents and caravans — a popular camping spot. Bright green succulents light up the floor of the **Barranco de la**

Above: view back over the Barranco de la Torre from the plain; left: the salt museum (open daily 09.30-17.30

Torre (**3**), and a sprinkling of palms dot the *barranco* a short way inland.

Twenty minutes from the restaurant you're on the beach at **Puerto de la Torre** (**4**; **1h15min**). (If you want to take a stroll up through the palms, the furthest stand is only 10 minutes away, but this detour is *not* included in the overall times.) To ascend out of the *barranco* and continue the walk, take the track veering off to the left. A short steep climb brings you up to a dusty plain littered with stones. Shortly you pass through the gateway of a rather broken down FENCE. Leave the track here (**a**), and follow the line of the fence to the clifftops, five minutes away. *(But for the Longer walk, continue on the track.)*

From here on the clifftops become your way, and you pass the remains of some HORNOS DE CAL (**5**; lime kilns). The sea below is a beautiful turquoise-green. Barely 15 minutes along the clifftops you come to the BIMBOY TRIG POINT on a jutting promontory (**6**; **1h40min**), from where there are beautiful views along the shoreline. Behind you, at the foot of the cliffs, a rocky shelf stretches out, and Caleta de Fuste is visible in the distance. Either turn back here or look ahead to what could be your last port of call on this walk — a small stony beach tucked back into this indented coastline.

A little over five minutes later, a gravel slide takes you down to the beach, at the mouth of the **Barranco de Majada Honda** (**1h45min**). It's a blissfully quiet spot. *Please note:* I have never swum at these beaches, so I do not know how safe they are. If you do intend to go swimming, please do so with the utmost care. As a rule, the beaches on this side of the island are considered safe.

The return follows the same route, and you're back at **Caleta de Fuste** approaching **3h30min**.

Walk 21: POZO NEGRO CIRCUIT VIA LA ATALAYITA

Distance: 8.5km/5.3mi; 1h30min
Grade: ● quite easy; the only ascent/descent is at the volcano halfway along (about 80m/250ft). Almost all along tracks in dry river beds, which can be rough at times. *Not waymarked,* but easily followed.
Equipment: trainers, light jacket, swimwear, sunhat, raingear, suncream, picnic, water
Transport: 🚗 to/from Pozo Negro; park at the end of the road (28° 19.452'N, 13° 53.732'W). Or 🚌 (Line 10) to the 'Saladillo' bus stop at the KM28 marker on the FV2, from where a track leads to the La Atalayita; begin and end the walk there (adds 3.5km return).

This easy walk leads via an aboriginal village with 115 different structures — and up a mini-volcano if you like. Time your visit to arrive when the Interpretation Centre is open (10.00-14.00), so you can make the most of the exhibition. The shaded picnic tables are always available.

Poblado La Atalayita

Start at Pozo Negro (○) by heading back towards the FV2, but then make your way into the DRY RIVER BED on the left, just below the road. Follow this to a motorable crossing track, turn left and walk to the **La Atalayita INTERPRETATION CENTRE (❶)** in the midst of the *malpais* ('badlands'; see page 23). Even without interpretation aids, it is easy to see how the earliest (pre-Conquest) inhabitants used the landscape to their advantage, creating dwellings of various designs and sizes and, most importantly, animal pens and corrals, from blocks of AA lava.

After visiting parts of the SETTLEMENT (❷), you may like to climb to the top of **La Atalayita** ('the little watchtower', for which the village was named; ❸) — for the view down over the layout and out to Pozo Negro and the sea. Then head back and turn left along another DRY RIVER BED — this one with a smoother track. You're back in **Pozo Negro (○) in 1h30min**, having followed in the footsteps of the early settlers, who had an inexhaustible supply of seafood protein here.

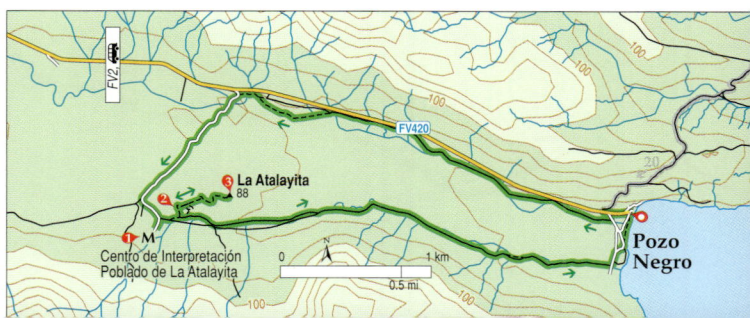

Walk 22: FROM GINIGINAMAR TO TARAJALEJO

Distance: 5.7km/3.5mi; 2h10min (add 4km/1h if travelling by bus)
Grade: ● ❗❗ moderate, with lots of dipping in and out of *barrancos*. There is no climbing to great heights; the overall ups and downs measure about 250m/820ft. But the path is rough and *vertiginous* — only recommended for adventurous, sure-footed walkers with a head for heights. *No shade*.
Equipment: walking boots, light jacket, sunhat, raingear, suncream, picnic, plenty of water
Transport: 🚌 to Giniginamar; park by the beach (28° 12.113'N, 14° 4.421'W). Or 🚐 (Line 01, 04, 10) to the Giniginamar turn-off, from where you must walk 4km/1h down the FV525 to Playa de Giniginamar to start the walk proper. Return on 🚐 from Tarajalejo (Lines 01, 04, 10), from where you will have to walk 4km down to Giniginamar (as above) if you left a car there.

Short walk: *Tarajalejo* (2km/1.2mi; 1h). ● Easy, but with a short, steep, gravelly descent to beach. Equipment as main walk, but sturdy shoes will suffice; access by 🚌 to/from Tarajalejo; park above the beach (28° 11.537'N, 14° 7.067'W). Or 🚐 to/from Tarajalejo (Lines 01, 04, 10). Follow the seaside road (Calle Isidro Diaz) east until it ends. Then turn right and immediately left. From here a track leads uphill to the coastal path (below a large cairn on the rise). Follow the path as it descends to a FIRST BEACH (**⑤**).

When you're tired of the beach and feel like getting those muscles working again, then I suggest this wild rugged coastal walk. However, it's not for everybody. If you're not the adventurous type, then the short walk should do nicely.

The walk starts at the BEACH in **Giniginamar** (**○**). (There are no buses here, but it's only an hour's walk (4km) down from the turn-off, otherwise take a taxi or ask friends to drop you off.) Head over to the little houses at the water's edge on the right-hand side of the beach, a few minutes along. Your path ascending the side of the ridge starts at the right-hand side of these houses. The steep stony path takes you up to the TOP OF THE RIDGE at **Punta del Morete** (**○**; **15min**). Now you have a lovely view back over this

Walk 22: From Giniginamar to Tarajalejo

predominantly fishing village, and back up into the *barranco*.

A little further along the coast opens up. Crests roll seaward and drop off into the sea. More crests and *barrancos* lie ahead, as you wend your way along the coast, dipping in and out of a succession of valleys, roller-coaster fashion. Ignore faint paths down to the sea. Soon you come upon a first (short) stretch of rocky descent down the side of a ridge, but this only takes a couple of minutes. Further along, rounding the next crest, you're overlooking a steep drop to the sea. The path is narrow — unnerving for anyone who doesn't have a head for heights.

Just over **30min** into the walk you reach a small stony beach at the mouth of a stream. Another, narrower *barranco* follows. Don't forget to look behind you as you cross here, for a fine view. Small piles of stones help mark the way … and seagulls have provided the white paint work! Two more small *barrancos* follow, as the still-vertiginous goats' path takes you

Sea horse on Tarajalejo's promenade

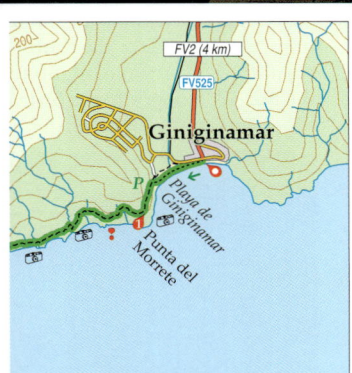

above the cliffs. It's a harsh environment you're crossing, the only noticeable vegetation being spiny *aulaga* and the odd hawthorne.

Some **55min** en route you encounter your only landmark — a large CONCRETE BLOCK in the middle of the path. Just beyond it another stretch of vertiginous path takes you around the steep flank of a hill. A small stony beach comes into sight below on the left. Here a short steep descent takes you down and across a wide stream bed, the **Barranco Morro Blanco** (❷).

Once across the *barranco,* without warning you're virtually balancing on a clifftop, with a beach (the **Playa del Caracol**; ❸) stretching out below you. (The fork off left here also goes down to the beach on the point.) Now several vertiginous path lead across the face of the hill: take the widest one and head above the beach; the paths all meet up a minute later. At the end of the beach, a short, slippery descent takes you down to another *barranco* crossing. Out of this (unnamed) stream bed the way veers inland. The fork left is a short-cut along a vertiginous path; keep right. You circle the top of a crest covered in CAIRNS (**1h20min**) — all passers-by have added to the collection. On the crest you meet a track: bear left, descending into the umpteenth *barranco.* A longish, steep ascent follows.

Seven minutes out of the stream bed, when the way forks, go right, away from the cliffs. Crossing another crest, you spot another beach below. At the fork that follows, descend to the left. This beach is accessible by vehicle, with tents and caravans about. It sits at the bottom of the very wide **Barranco de Marquina Yosa** (❹), which fans out as it approaches the sea. Note that these beaches drop away very abruptly into deep water.

At the end of the *playa* your track ascends the hillside. Ignore all other tracks. Looking back across the valley from here, you suddenly realise how large it is — an amphitheatre of hills circling back to the coast, and within it are more hills and valleys. You cross another track on the top of the crest, and dip down into your last *barranco* and *playa* (❺; **1h45min**), from where you continue on a path. A steep climb takes you out of the *barranco,* and paths fork off in all directions. Basically they're all okay, as long as you don't veer inland, but I suggest the higher path that heads round the hillside, not the one near the shore. Tracks head off here in all directions.

The beach at Tarajalejo appears … then the resorts and the urbanization up in the valley and, finally, tucked into the hillside, the village itself comes out of hiding. After crossing a track, you join another track descending a crest, meet up with the lower path, and head over towards the houses.

Coming into **Tarajalejo** (**2h05min**), ignore the first two streets to the right. (Opposite the first street is a minuscule 'port', where a few colourful fishing boats make a focal point for photos of the sea. The village also has a very pleasant promenade, with some fun sculptures.) Take the third right, the wide main road, up to the BUS STOP opposite the Spar supermarket (❻; **2h10min**).

Right, Walk 23: on the pilgrims' path to the Ermita Virgin del Tanquito. Many paths on the island are marked out like this one and the one on page 53, with stones at the sides.

Walk 23: MONTAÑA CARDÓN

See also photo on page 41
Distance: 4.3km/2.7mi; 1h30min
Grade: ● easy-moderate ascent/descent of 190m/625ft; signed and green/white waymarked SL FV 53
Equipment: walking shoes/boots (somewhat skiddy trail), light jacket, sunhat, suncream, water, optional picnic
Transport: 🚌 Take the FV605 from Pájara towards La Pared and turn left after 11km on the FV618, signposted to Cardón. After 3km park in a layby on the left (east side of the road), where signposts

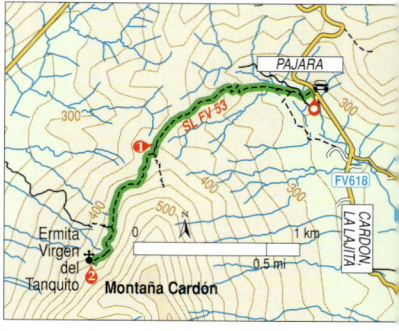

indicate the walk (28° 16.425'N, 14° 8.975'W). *No bus access*

This short walk is ideal for a morning or afternoon constitutional: you follow a pilgrims' path to a mountaintop chapel. Early on, an information board describes the area's centuries of legends and history.

Start out at the PARKING AREA on the FV618 (○). Follow the fingerpost for 'EL TANQUITO', crossing straight over a dirt track some 100m below the road and passing a DAM that holds the water from the confluence of the two *barrancos* at this point. Walk down into the stream bed and up the other side to an INFORMATION BOARD about the mountain and the Virgin of El Tanquito.

From here we follow the PILGRIMS' TRAIL up the mountain to a ridge and a SADDLE marked by a wooden pole (❶) — a lovely viewpoint over a large part of the island. Up ahead is the jagged Cardón massif, and all around is desert vegetation: *tabobo* (wild tobacco, *Nicotiana glauca*), *Euphorbia*, *Kleinia nerisfolia* and the spikey shrubs on which goats feast.

The rest of your walk is easily seen: the path ahead is somewhat steeper. Soon you look out over the sandy desert of El Jable (Walks 24 and 25) and beyond it the mountains of the Jandía Peninsula. Go through a GATE and a minute later come to a large INFORMATION BOARD about the **Monumento Natural de Montaña Cardón**. It's just a few minutes more to a picnic site with an old oven, primitive grills, and a *galería* (a tunnel bored for water extraction). Thirty metres further on you come to the *ermita* of the **Virgen del Tanquito** (❷; **50min**) with a natural spring and a small freshwater pond.

Ignoring the trail continuing on from the chapel, retrace your steps back to the PARKING AREA (○).

Walk 24: THE PARED ISTHMUS

Distance: 12.5km/7.8mi; 3h15min
Grade: 🔵 easy. The walk crosses a sandy plain on tracks. One steep, slippery descent lasting a few minutes, and a steep 15min climb up a sandhill; overall ups and downs of about 200m/650ft. Don't attempt on very windy days, when all the sand in the air will make it extremely unpleasant.
Equipment: comfortable walking shoes, fleece, sunhat, suncream, sunglasses, rainwear, picnic, plenty of water

Transport: 🚗 to/from Costa Calma; park at El Palmeral shopping centre (28° 7.711'N, 14° 13.798'W). Or 🚌 (Lines 01, 04, 05, 09, 10) to/from Costa Calma; alight at the bus stop called 'Gasolinera Costa Calma', just south of the petrol station and the El Palmeral shopping centre.
Shorter walk: Aqua Liques (10km/6.2mi; 2h30min). 🔵 Grade, access and equipment as main walk. Follow the main walk to **Aqua Liques** (❸), then return the same way.

Y ou start off this hike with the giant wind generators stealing your attention, then you cross the sandy isthmus to the spellbinding sea and its glaring cliffs and rolling dunes. If you're staying anywhere in the vicinity then this walk is a must. It's a popular excursion, so you needn't worry about finding your way. However, tracks criss-cross this isthmus in all directions, and the route could easily change in the near future. *Basically as long as you **head straight over the isthmus**, you can't get lost.*

Start out at the EL PALMERAL shopping centre at **Costa Calma** (❶). Walk uphill on the road just to the right of the shopping centre (with the 'no entry' sign), passing the Restaurante Mediterran on the right. Minutes up, you're away from the resort. In front of you lies a sandy plain that stretches into nothingness. But before you notice anything else, you'll be spellbound by rows of wind generators over to your left. Not only are they a work of art (or perhaps you beg to differ!), but they blend into the landscape. They're striking in their simplicity.

About five minutes along, when the road heads right, continue ahead. Your walk across

The spectacular seascape near the point, Los Boquetes

Walk 24: The Pared isthmus

the isthmus is straight on, but first you have to take a detour to cross the motorway. Turn right on a track here (by a PYLON) and follow it until you can turn left to cross the motorway via an UNDERPASS (❶; **10min**). Once on the far side, turn left until you are back opposite the pylon, then head right on a clear track. Far to the right you can see the jagged hills that enclose the Tarajalejo Valley, where Walk 22 ends. To the left, the 'hills' are barely ripples in the landscape. The faint whining sound of wind generators permeates the air.

You'll see other walkers crossing the isthmus. All on different tracks. But don't panic, you *are* on one of the tracks that will get you there — even if it's covered with sand from time to time. Eventually you cross the signposted **GR 131** (❷; **35min**) and the sea comes into view. After leaving another track off to the right you're almost there — perhaps being battered by the wind. The island seems to roll straight off into the sea — the cliffs are still in hiding. To your left is the piercing mountain chain that rears up along the Jandía Peninsula.

Several faint tracks now cross your way and you continue straight on. Beyond ONE MORE WIDE TRACK (which you follow to the right for just a few paces), you're above the sea at **Aqua Liques** (❸; **1h15min**). A bite in the cliffs allows you to — *carefully!* — slide your way down to the shore in just a few minutes. A rocky sea-ledge sitting just above the water, at the foot of the cliffs, enables you to walk quite a long way along the shoreline. This seascape is exquisite, with its brilliant blue waters, dark lava-coloured rocks and off-white, rose-tinted cliffs of fossilized sand.

Walks 24 and 25 both skirt below these wind generators. Some of you won't agree with me, but they are one of my favourite sights on the island!

Your immediate destination is the point along to the right, where the cliffs subside into sandhills. This coastal walk is nothing short of spectacular. On hazeless days you can see the Jandía Peninsula curving out to your left. Barbary ground squirrels scurry to and fro amongst the rocks. Not far along you come to a small sandy beach. A knee dip is about all I can recommend here … it's the usual story: dangerous undertows. Nearing the point, sandhills roll back off the shore. Stunted *aulaga* and large-thorned *espinos* grow

You pass this colourful display as you travel to La Pared on the FV2: it's the Oasis Park, hiding a wildlife centre and botanical gardens.

rampant on these dunes. The waves crashing over the shoreline rocks are an awesome sight. Closer to the point, notice the dark red hues emanating from the sea-cliffs below you. A little under 45 minutes along the sea ledge you pass a SANDY TRACK rising to the right and then you're at the point, **Los Boquetes** (4; **2h**). A few minutes further on, a dramatic rock wall blocks your way. Don't venture too close to the sea here!

Homeward bound, go back to the sandy track and follow it to the left. It forks almost at once; go left again, rising up to the plateau. When you meet a crossing track after about 10 minutes, turn right. After less than 400m (you may have passed a BLUE POST about halfway along), be sure to leave this wide track for a narrower track that rises up to a low ridge, where you can get your bearings. Your target from here is the wooded park-like area behind Costa Calma, which is now in sight.

You cross the **GR 131** (5) again, then continue straight on along the **Cañada del Río** (6), the stream bed below, sometimes on a track marked with cairns. On reaching the motorway embankment, follow the fence downhill for about 150m to another (well hidden) UNDERPASS (7). Go through the tunnel, then turn left and head back up the hill on another dirt road to pick up your original route opposite where the motorway intersected it. Turn right for 120m, to a small ROUNDABOUT (**3h05min**).

Keep straight ahead through the urbanization. On coming to another ROUNDABOUT just past the Royal Suite Hotel, you'll find the BUS STOP (for those travelling south) to the right (**3h15min**). If you're heading north, go past this bus stop and, at the following roundabout, go right. Go left at the fourth roundabout, then cross the main road. Your BUS STOP (8) is ahead, in front of the Hotel Fuerteventura Playa. (If you came by car to Costa Calma, you can either walk the 2km back to the El Palmeral shopping centre by keeping straight ahead at the fourth roundabout, or catch a southbound bus to the 'GASOLINERA' BUS STOP.)

Walk 25: EL JABLE

See also photos on pages 108 and 124-125
Distance: 21.6km/13.4mi; 6h
Grade: 🔴 relatively easy if it's not too windy, but moderate on account of the length. Turn back if you encounter strong winds — it will be very unpleasant otherwise, as much of the walk is through sand dunes (and sand sometimes blows over the tracks, hiding them altogether). A drawn out ascent of 200m/650ft; ups and downs of 350m/1150ft overall. *No shade.*
Equipment: comfortable shoes, fleece, sunhat, suncream, sunglasses, raingear, picnic, plenty of water
Transport: 🚗 to/from Costa Calma; park at El Palmeral shopping centre (28° 7.711'N, 14° 13.798'W). Or 🚌 (Lines 01, 04, 05, 09, 10) to/from Costa Calma; alight at the bus stop called 'Gasolinera Costa Calma', just south of the petrol station and the El Palmeral shopping centre.

Alternative walk: From El Palmeral to the Barranco de Pecenescal and Risco del Paso (16.5/10.3mi; 4h45min). 🔴 Grade (about 200m/650ft of ascent/descent), equipment, access as the main walk. Return on 🚌 (Lines 01, 05) from the Barranco de Pecenescal — back to base, or back to your car at Costa Calma. **Start out** by following **Walk 24**. When the GR 131 cuts across in front of you (**❷**; **35min**), turn left. You will now follow the GR for about 6km/3.8mi — in the opposite direction to the main walk. At the **Degollada de Mojones** (**❺**; **2h20min**), the GR turns left and descends into the large valley ahead. Not far downhill, where the main track/GR heads down right into the *barranco,* you could keep left (a short-cut), soon rejoining the main track in the stream bed. About six minutes later, you leave the *barranco* and bear right round the slopes of a hill (**Atalayeja Grande**). More of the valley opens up, and the sea is in sight. Shortly you cross the bed of the wide **Barranco Tras del Lomo** (**ⓐ**; **2h50min**) that comes down from the right. Minutes later, the track loops back into the **Barranco de Pecenescal** (**ⓑ**), joining the SL FV 11. Looking up the side-valley, a herders' outpost comes into view — the **Casas de Pecenescal**. Loma Negra is the mountain that fills the left side of the valley. Reaching the main FV2 motorway, follow the GR under the motorway

Walk 25: El Jable

bridge. You join a cycle path on the far side: follow it to the left for just over 700m/about half a mile, to a roundabout on the *old* FV2, which descends to Risco del Paso. Your BUS STOP (**C**; **4h45min**) is at the roundabout. Or just follow the GR 131 down the *barranco* to **Risco del Paso** (**d**).

Shorter walk: Barranco de Pecenescal — Degollada de Mojones — Barranco de Pecenescal (11km/6.8mi; 2h55min). ● Moderate ascent of 150m/500ft overall.

Equipment as above; 🚗 or 🚐 to Exit 73 on the FV2 motorway, where there is a ROUNDABOUT with BUS STOP (**C**) on the old FV2 road. Alight at the roundabout; park by the recycling bins just a bit further along the old road (28° 7.590'N, 14° 16.318'W). From the roundabout take the cycle path west, then follow the GR 131 under the motorway and up to the **Degolada de Mojones.** Return the same way. Be prepared for strong winds at the pass!

Unique on the island! A walk through *real* sand dunes, not like the tame dunes at Corralejo. And should you strike a wind, which is the usual case, you'll think you're crossing the Sahara. If heading through a sand-dust storm doesn't sound like your cup of tea, give this hike a miss. I strongly recommend it, however. (The Shorter walk gives you the chance to turn back, if it's far too windy.)

Start out by following WALK 24 on page 92, crossing the **GR 131** (**2**; **35min**) and eventually — about 200m beyond a final WIDE TRACK — arriving at **Aqua Liques** (**3**; **1h15min**). Enjoy the spectacular coastal view over sand-encrusted cliffs, lava rock and white-capped waves. A bite in the cliffs allows you to — *carefully!* — slide your way down to the shore in just a few minutes.

A rocky sea-ledge sitting just above the water, at the foot of the cliffs, enables you to walk quite a long way along the shoreline. Walk 24 follows this ledge to the right, towards Los Boquetes. But this walk heads along to the left. After about 1km, where it's less steep, leave the ledge and take a faint path up to the left, ignoring all offshoots down towards the sea. Soon you come back up to the WIDE TRACK you crossed earlier before Aqua Liques. (If you miss this path, don't worry — just keep to the ledge and head up to the track further west wherever convenient — you don't need a path.)

Now following this track

View north from Playa Risco del Paso towards Atalayeja Grande and Loma Negra. The Alternative walk can end at Risco del Paso, descending via the Barranco de Pecenescal/GR 131 and dipping down to the splendid beach shown on pages 124-125.

112 Landscapes of Fuerteventura

westwards, you have a good outlook along the formidable barrier of mountains that run along the peninsula from here — if haze or sand dust doesn't obliterate your view! If it's going to be windy, you'll know by now — and it will get much worse once you're crossing the open dunes! A steady climb lies ahead, with tracks and paths joing you from the left and right. At **1h50min** a track joins you from the left, and the way levels out. Rounding a hill, you

Walk 25: El Jable 113

have an impressive view across the dunes and may be surprised to find *taboire (Ononis hebecarpa)* growing on the hillsides. In spring it is quite a sight, with bright yellow blooms.

Just before getting into the dunes proper, it's a good idea to you have a fine view over the beach of Barlovento and the crags of Jandía rearing up just ahead.

Then return to the main route and follow BLUE POLE MARKERS to the **Degollada de Mojones** (**5**; **3h20min**). Meeting a T-junction

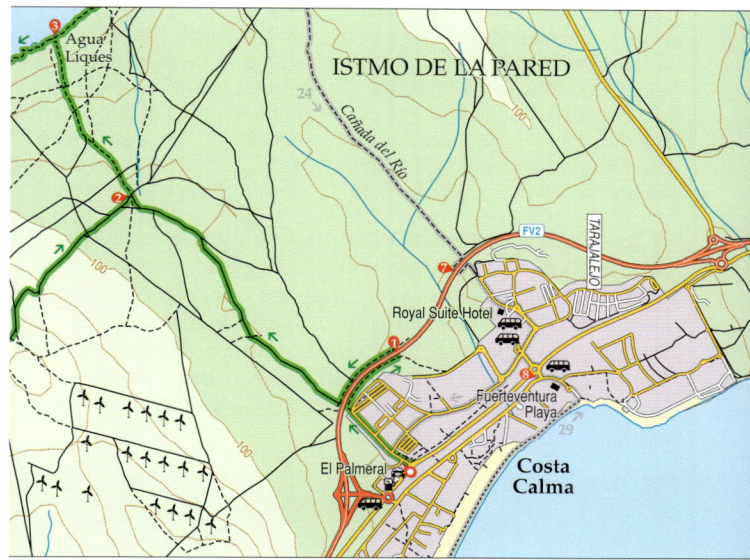

get your bearings from this height, especially if visibility is low and you can't see any of the tracks! (Don't worry. The whole idea is to continue from here approximately parallel to the coast; then, when the sand dunes of **El Jable** make way for other terrain — like darker rock — walk 90° inland. This way you cannot get lost.)

Once over a side-crest, another sloping valley awaits you. One last crest is crossed at about **2h30min**. Some 10 minutes later, shortly before the start of the Jandía mountains, you'll spot your faint route heading left uphill. However, if conditions are good, first detour to the gravelly HILLOCK over to the right (**4**; **2h50min**), from where

at this pass, go left towards a ridge, passing a sign asking you not to leave the main trail, as this is a protected area for birds. You're now on the **GR 131** which runs slightly below the ridge — an old stone-paved 'road' — you may see the paving below patches of sand.

About 40 minutes from the pass the wind turbines above Costa Calma come back into view. Further along this high-level route you pass to the right of **Alto de Água Oveja** and about half an hour later you're back at the GR crossroads you met on the outward route (**2**; **5h30min**). Retrace your steps from here to the EL PALMERAL shopping centre at **Costa Calma** (**O**; **6h**).

Walk 26: PICO DE LA ZARZA

Distance: 15.6km/9.7mi; 5h
Grade: ● strenuous, with an ascent of 820m/2690ft. The ascent is nearly all on a track, except for the last 25min, where you follow a path to the summit. It can be very hot — or very cold and windy. Not recommended on very windy days — nor on cloudy days, since the climb is only worth it for the view and, if you were lost in mist, the climb could be dangerous as well. But everyone who is fit should try this hike, beginners included. Well waymarked with the yellow/white flashes of the PR FV 54
Equipment: walking boots or stout shoes with ankle support, warm jacket, raingear, sunhat, suncream, picnic, plenty of water
Transport: 🚗 to/from the Ventura Shopping Centre at Jandía Playa, where there is a large car park (28° 3.172'N, 14° 19.424'W) — or you could park (as most walkers do) on the track below the water tank 10 minutes uphill (28° 3.555'N, 14° 19.699'W). Or 🚐 (Lines 01, 04, 05, 09, 10) to/from the Ventura Shopping Centre

Pico de la Zarza is Fuerteventura's highest peak and worth climbing for two reasons: the grand panorama that tumbles away below you and the wealth of botanical specimens to be seen en route. The best time to scale this mountain is in spring, when the summit is resplendent with yellow-flowering *Asteriscus* (see below). But, be warned: it can be very windy! On a calm day, it's one of the most exhilarating spots on the island.

Walk 26: Pico de la Zarza

The walk starts at the BUS STOP (⭕) in front of the VENTURA SHOPPING CENTRE. Follow the FV2 a short way east, to the ROUNDABOUT with the tall modern sculpture. Turn left here and walk up the wide road beside the Occidental Jandía Playa Hotel. After 300m/yds, turn left on CALLE SANCHO PANZA (above a road left to the 'Mini Golf'). As this road bends round to the right and edges the **Barranco de Vinamar**, aim for a large white WATER TANK you can see up ahead. When the road forks, keep right and right again on a track a minute later, to pass to the right of this WATER TANK (❶). Nearby is a WALKERS' INFORMATION BOARD for the **PR FV 54**.

Follow the track uphill; it quickly becomes rough and winds its way up the rock- and stone-strewn slopes. You pass to the right of twin-peaked **Talahijas**; its lower summit can be quickly reached, but for the ascent of Zarza a stiff climb lies ahead. Meanwhile, you already have a superb view back over the long white Playa del Matorral with its turquoise-green shoreline. The Barranco de Vinamar, as bleak as the rest of the countryside, cuts straight back into the massif.

Climbing higher, you catch sight of corrals hidden in the depths of the ravine. On heading round to the eastern side of the ridge, you overlook another harsh valley (**Valluelo de la Cal**, with a stone quarry and rubbish dump), where more ridges hint at a succession of ravines in the distance. You have an excellent view that stretches to the hills at the centre of the island. Pico de la Zarza is the unimpressive peak that rises a thumbnail above the rest of the massif at the very end of this ridge.

Reaching the cloud zone, you find that the top of the crest is very herbaceous. It's quite a wild garden! (Keep well clear of any goats you may encounter up here; they are very easily frightened and will dart off in all directions if startled; in particular, avoid any with kids.) Climbing higher, you head alongside a bouldery crest, flooded with *tabaiba* bushes, *verode* and asphodels. Look, too, down on the *barranco* walls below, where you'll spot some enormous *candelabra*. When the track reaches about 500m/1640ft (**2h**) it deteriorates. The track stops dead on the crest of the ridge

From the summit of Pico de la Zarza, you look out towards the tip of the Jandía Peninsula. There's a surprising amount of greenery up here, including the furry-leafed yellow Asteriscus, *an island endemic.*

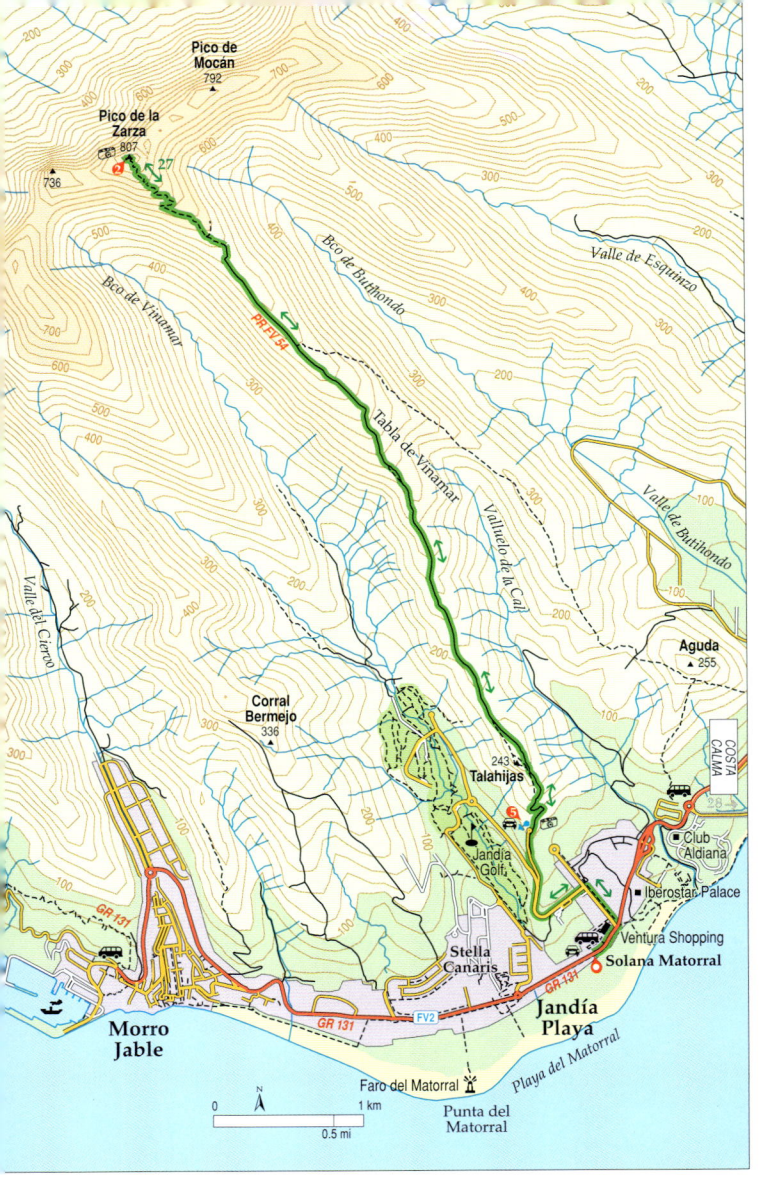

(**2h35min**), leaving you to continue to the top on a good path. *Lamarzkia aurea* (it resembles the bottle-brush plant) flourishes up here, and soon the slopes are ablaze with golden yellow *Asteriscus*. About 200m/yds from the summit, the environmental authorities have erected a high fence, to protect the very special flora from goats and sheep. There used to be a gate in the fence, but it's been just a gap for several years.

Eventually, windswept and exhausted, you're on the roof of

The rocky summit of Zarza, with the dilapidated fence and 'gate' (photo taken in November, when the Asteriscus *were not in bloom*

the island, atop **Pico de la Zarza** (❷; **3h**). And what a view! To the left you look across the lofty crags that rupture this impenetrable wall of rock. The jutting southwestern coastline unfolds as this barrier of mountains dies down into sand-patched hills and finally a sea-plain. Don't venture too near to the edge of the peak; it plummets hundreds of feet straight down onto a sea-flat.

The mysterious mansion with a turret visited on Walk 27 sits back off the flat, in the shadows of the cliffs — the Cortijo de Cofete (or 'Villa Winter': read about its history in Walks 18 and 27). More in keeping with the landscape is Cofete, the hamlet over to the left. To your right stand the high rolling sandhills of the Pared isthmus that joins these mountains to the northern half of the island. On hazeless days, it's possible to see well down the eastern coastline to Lanzarote.

Botanists will want to tarry here on the summit for quite some time to discover more of the island's floral treasures: *Echium handiense, Bupleurum handiense, Sideritis massoniana, Argyranthemum winteri,* and the more common *Ranunculus cortusifolius, Andryala cheiranthifolia* and *Minuartia platyphylla*. The summit also housed a tiny meteorological hut — now in ruins — and two large antennae.

Home is all downhill — sheer bliss — two hour's descent away. You'll be back at the VENTURA SHOPPING CENTRE (◯) in about **5h**.

Walk 27: FROM BARRANCO GRAN VALLE TO COFETE

See also photos on pages 15, 26-17 and the cover
Distance: 7.5km/4.7mi; 2h30min
Grade: ● moderate-strenuous, with a ascent of 300m/985ft to the pass (Degollada de Cofete). The path on the west coast is rocky and stony. It can be very hot, and there is *no shade*. The beach is usually very windy. The walk (waymarked PR FV 55) is accessible to all.
Equipment: walking boots, warm fleece, sunhat, raingear, suncream, swimwear, picnic, plenty of water
Transport: 🚗 to/from Barranco Gran Valle: take the road signed for 'Punta de Jandía' on the west side of Morro Jable. After about 3km you pass a water tank on the left, 40m beyond which the GR 131 crosses the road. Some 450m further on, there is a car park/bus stop at an info board for the PR FV 55 (28° 3.806'N, 14° 22.571'W). Or 🚌 111 from Morro Jable station to the 'Gran Valle' stop. Return on 🚌 Line 111 from Cofete or Playa de Cofete — back to your car or back to Morro Jable.

Cross the Jandía Peninsula to the isolated west coast and see what isolated really means. The inviting beaches and crashing breakers are enough to send anyone running down to meet them! This walk may well prove to be your favourite on the island: climbing to the windy saddle, where Cofete Beach and the Villa Winter open out below, is unforgettable.

The walk begins at the entrance to **Barranco Gran Valle**, where a clear path begins by the INFO BOARD shown overleaf for the **PR FV 55** (●). From here head straight into the ravine. Standing at the entrance to this austere *barranco,* you can see all the way to the end of it. A settlement of stone corrals sits at the foot of the lofty summits. On either side of you the valley floor sweeps back up into severe rocky walls. Out here you meet only goats, sheep ... and, nowadays, hikers. Keep an eye out for the rare cactus-like *Euphorbia handiensis* (Jandía cactus spurge,

Playa de Cofete (see also cover photo) is a glorious sweep of sand. There's a cemetery just next to the beach developed in the 19th century by the first settlers. At the right of the 'door' to the cemetery are the names of the people buried here — their family names attesting to much inbreeding as the result of the isolation of the area.

Walk 27: From Barranco Gran Valle to Cofete

photo on page 129) on this walk. It only grows in a few places south of Morro Jable. The only other vegetation in this stony terrain is the tobacco plant, *cosco, Lycium intricatum,* and *aulaga*.

You quickly reach the hamlet of **La Solana** (❶; **5min**), with pens for goats, poultry and other livestock constructed out of everything from fishing nets to metal. At the same time you cross a track leading to Casas de Gran Valle with its many rock-built corrals. Continue on the well-defined, manicured footpath, passing above an EARTHEN-WALLED DAM — no doubt dry.

Further into the valley you're looking out onto the tired stone pens of **Casas de Gran Valle**, the old pastoral outpost you could see from the start of the walk. In the past this area was an aboriginal settlement; some of their small stone dwellings are still clearly visible.

You cross a couple of dry side-streams before the real ascent begins. At the foot of the pass the way (once the main route across the peninsula, now restored) swings back to the right to begin a zigzag ascent. A grassy plant, *Lamarzkia aurea,* flanks the path. Nearing the col, you cross a colourful bare rock-face. Keeping to the right-hand side of the pass, you cross the **Degollada de Cofete** (❷; **1h20min**) and look up at towering crags that stand like sentries on either side. The pointed peak on the left is called **Fraile**. Stretching out below you are the striking golden beaches of Cofete (left) and Barlovento de Jandía

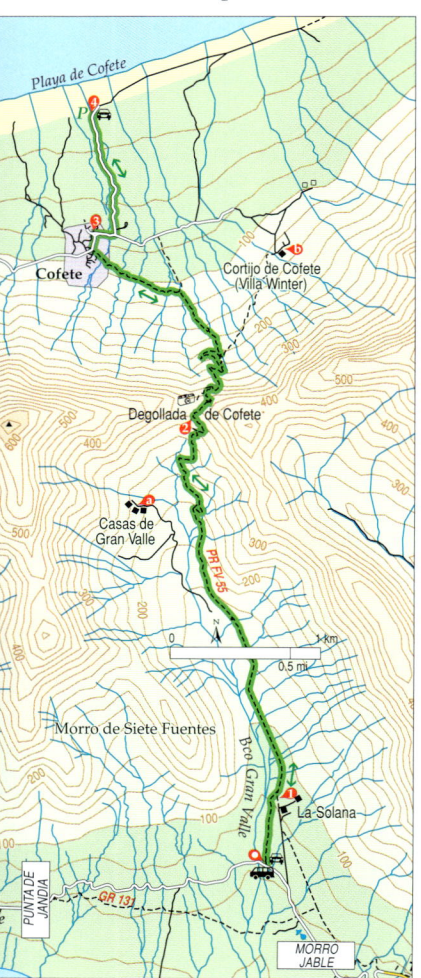

(right). A bizarrely-sited chateau-like villa with a turret, the CORTIJO DE COFETE (also called 'Villa Winter') immediately captures your attention. Legends abound about this house, so lets visit it and make up our own minds. Cofete is the outpost of stone and cement-block huts nearby, its ugliness eclipsed by the dazzling stretch of coastline.

Below the pass the good clear path, sometimes hewn from the rock, continues down to the right. The lichen-flecked pinnacles of rock that pierce this range keep drawing your attention. This chain of volcanic mountains harbours the island's most interesting flora. Behind you, the *riscos* (cliffs) rise up into dark sinister shadows.

Accompanied by large, but friendly, yellow grasshoppers, some 45 minutes below the pass you come to a crossing track (**3**; **2h10min**). Here you *could* follow the path directly towards the houses and huts of Cofete. But instead fork right to the **Cortijo de Cofete** (**4**) where, for a symbolic contribution of €1-2, you can enter and have an individual tour. It belonged to a Sr Winter, a German engineer who came to the island before World War II and eventually owned the entire peninsula. When the house was built in the early 1940s, he forbade his workers (or anyone, for that matter) to live in Cofete. Everyone had to return to Morro Jable at the end of the day. Obviously stories grew about the place (which would have been a good setting for a Hitchcock film!) The house is now an unofficial 'museum', inhabited by the grandson of one of the original labourers. (The bar/restaurant in Cofete was built by the same company as the villa — notice the similarity of the walls.)

After your visit make the short descent to the the fort-like bar/restaurant downhill in **Cofete** (**5**; **2h50**) itself for some refreshment, then head back east for a few metres along the track, keep left at a fork, and head straight down to **Playa de Cofete** (**6**; **3h05min**) and the adjacent CEMETERY. Expect company: this side of the peninsula has been well and truly 'discovered'

Walk 27: From Barranco Gran Valle to Cofete 121

— but there's still plenty of beach for everyone. Remember that the undertow here is treacherous, and swimming would be foolhardy!

Important: The return minibus 111 leaves the beach daily at about 16.45, and it is best you try to pick it up at the beach BUS STOP. If you go to the bar/restaurant, where there is another stop, it may already be full! Unless some Good Samaritan will give you a lift to

Top left and clockwise: breathtaking view from the Degollada de Cofete down over the mysterious Villa Winter; the villa seen from the goat enclosure adjacent to Cofete's bar/restaurant; kiosk at the villa 'museum', showing opening times and asking for upkeep donations; the start of the walk in Gran Valle, with the 'manicured' path, delineatede with stones; a colony of Euphorbias *near Cofete*

Morro Jable, you may have to walk back over the pass…

WALK 28: FROM MORRO JABLE TO COSTA CALMA ALONG THE BEACH

Distance: 13km/8mi; 3h40min
Grade: ● easy, almost flat, but walking continuously on sand is tiring. Don't attempt on a fairly windy day, when it could be very unpleasant.
Equipment: sandals, long sleeved shirt, sunhat, suncream, sunglasses, swimwear, picnic, plenty of water

Transport: 🚗 to the Hotel Meliá Fuerteventura south of Costa Calma; park near the hotel (28° 8.262'N, 14° 14.669'W). From there (or from your base) take a 🚌 to Club Aldiana (Lines 01, 04, 05, 09, 10) to start the walk. The walk ends at the Hotel Meliá, where you pick up your car or return to

base. Check the Tiadhe webside in advance (which may refer to the hotel by its old name, Gorriones): not all buses stop at the hotel itself; you may have to walk 20min up to the hotel turn-off on the FV2.

Beach, beer, and bare bods: that's what this walk is all about. This is the stretch of coastline that has made Fuerteventura famous. Take the bare minimum with you; a number of small bars en route make perfect refueling stations. If you're expecting solitude, forget it — but there's plenty of space for everyone on Playa de Sotavento de Jandía. Make a day of it.

The walks starts at the CLUB ALDIANA ROUNDABOUT (**6**). Take the road on the north side of the complex and make your way down to the beach, and you're away — passing the first bar immediately. Since so many people either build their own stone wind shelter here, or add to the ones they've bought, this beach tends to look like an archeogical site of old Guanche ruins. And did I mention: clothes *off* is the rule rather than the exception on this stretch of coastline?

When this beach ends, you

123

clamber over stones to continue along the next one — a large bay with a narrow beach, the **Playa de Butihondo** (❶). This umbrella and sunbed beach, with several bars thrown in, runs past the **Esquinzo** resort (❷). Crossing stones and rounding a sandhill at **Boca de Esquinzo** (❸), you're into your third beach — another fortification of stone-built shelters. Flags hoisted means occupied: find your own wind-shelter!

Mass tourism is behind you now. The further north you go, the more beautiful the beaches. Leaving the bay behind, you cross a stretch of rocks, and look up into a *barranco* free of buildings. Around the corner lies another equally beautiful beach, with just a few sunbeds and brollies. **Club Tierra Dorada** (❹; **1h30min**) sits on the hillside above. Towards the end of this beach you can quench your thirst at another bar. On clear days the island's midriff, the hilly interior, can be seen curving around to the right from here, and a collar of sand leads the eye along to another beach. Two long arms of dunes run down to this next beach, at the mouth of the **Barranco de Pecenescal** (Walk 27). **El Paso** (253m) is the hill ahead that outsizes all the others. A small corner of houses at the end of the *playa* (❺; **Casas Risco del Paso**) is the only damage done here.

Past these houses, you come upon *the jewel* — **Playa de Sotavento de Jandía** (**2h10min**): it's on the cover of every tourist brochure. Ahead is a sweeping sand bar with tidal lagoons. When the tide is out, this sandy promontory extends several hundred metres out from the shore, and you can make your way along it (otherwise, just follow the shore). A small beach bar appears below a rocky protrusion. The *HOTEL MELIA FUERTEVENTURA* is the eyesore on this stretch of coastline — but at least it calls your attention to the nearest bus stop. In the distance to the left, a few of the nearby wind generators come into sight. The shoreline sea is a beryl green; beyond, it's deep blue. At **3h30min** you're level with the hotel. If you're ready to call it a day, then go no further. Walk over to the bus stop by the **Hotel Meliá** (❻; **3h40min**). *But note:* the bus company may still refer to the hotel by its old name, Gorriones, and not all buses call in here; you

Playa de Sotavento de Jandía at Risco del Paso (Walks 28 and 29): this spot, with its sand bar, is mesmerisingly beautiful at high tide.

may have to walk 20 minutes uphill, past the hotel, to the FV2.

Or, if you're still enjoying the walk, refer to the map above: the Costa Calma beach lies another hour away, and the nearest bus stop 25 minutes beyond it. Just keep on along the sand bar, then follow the coast. Three more pretty coves, full of naked souls, lie on route. If the tide is high, take the track above the sea, then descend to the main beach. At Costa Calma, those heading north will find their BUS STOP (7) behind the **Fuerteventura Playa Hotel**, at the end of the beach. If you're southbound, take the road from that hotel up to the main road. Cross over, and at the next roundabout, find the BUS STOP (8) just opposite — off to the right.

WALK 29: THE SOTAVENTO LAGOON

The map is on page 123 and the main photo on pages 124-125. Waypoint numbers correspond to those for Walk 28.
Distance: 8.7km/5.4mi; 2h45min-3h
Grade: 🔵 very easy, almost flat — but walking on sand can be tiring. Don't attempt on a windy day, when it could be very unpleasant.
Note: Obviously the best time to go is when there is water in the lagoon at high tide; otherwise there won't be a sand bar! Check the tide tables in advance at wisuki.com (which has a webcam).

Equipment: sandals, sunhat, suncream, sunglasses, long sleeved shirt, swimwear, picnic, plenty of water
Transport: 🚗 to/from the Hotel Meliá Fuerteventura south of Costa Calma; park near the hotel (28° 8.262'N, 14° 14.669'W). Or 🚌 (Lines 01, 04, 05, 09, 10) to/from the Hotel Gorriones. Check the Tiadhe webside in advance: not all buses stop at the hotel itself (which Tiadhe may still refer to by its old name, Gorriones); you may have to alight/reboard on the FV2, at the hotel turn-off.

If Sotavento de Jandía is one of the most attractive beaches in Europe, it's not only the soft white sand that sets it apart. At high tide the sea fills the very shallow lagoon (shown on pages 124-125) — almost four kilometres long and a good 200 metres wide — framed by a long narrow sand bar. (At low tide, when the lagoon is dry, you'll have trouble even *finding* it …) This walk is highly recommended as a circuit, heading out along the sand bar and back along the coast — where you may be able to potter about in tidal pools and mud flats, scattering fish… Don't forget to bring some peanuts, too for the barbary ground squirrels (you may have met some already on one one of the other walks — Walk **5** particularly); they will want to be eating out of your hand.

The walk begins at the HOTEL MELIA FUERTEVENTURA (**6**), from where you follow signs past a large CAR PARK and the 'KITE CENTER' and down to glorious **Playa Barca** — the northeastern part of **Playa de Sotavento de Jandía**. Even when the parking areas are all bursting at the seams, you will never feel crowded on this beach.

Then head south along the SAND BAR, sometimes wading through channels where the sand bar is broken. (Be aware that, depending on the season and the tides, these can be over a metre/four feet deep!) There is a particularly wide channel just before **Playa Risco del Paso** (**5**; **1h30min**) at the southern end of the lagoon — arguably the most beautiful part of the walk. There used to be a bar (serving drinks, not a sand bar …) here until very recently, and it is sorely missed!

From here just carry on northwards along the shore — perhaps lowering your eyes in the company of the many naturists who frequent this part of the beach, but most of all enjoying the antics of the windsurfs and kitesurfs and dipping in and out of the sea.

Walk 30: TIP OF THE ISLAND

Distance: 11.5km/7.1mi; 3h20min
Grade: ● moderate, with overall ascents of just under 200m/650ft on tracks and sandy paths. Signed, yellow/white waymarked PR FV 56; the last hour red/white waymarked GR 131
Equipment: comfortable shoes, fleece, bathing things, sunhat, suncream, sunglasses, picnic, plenty of water
Transport: 🚗 to/from Puertito de la Cruz (28° 4.416'N, 14° 30.008'W). Or 🚐 (Line 111): departs Morro Jable 10.00; returns from Puertito de la Cruz at about 16.00

This walk won't suit everyone: it's a very long drive from anywhere unless you're based around Morro Jable, the first hour is spent slogging across desert and the last hour is also fairly boring. But … the middle part of the walk, with impressive views of the tip of the island, the Jandía Peninsula and El Jable is simply spectacular.

Start out at **Puertito de la Cruz** (**O**) in the middle of nowhere, with its single wind turbine. Just opposite the BUS STOP, take the sandy track signposted 'PLAYA DE LA MADERA', with mountains on your right and cliffs on your left. Not far along you come to the sandy beach of **Playa de Ojos** (**❶**; 20min). A trail leads down to it. A few minutes later you pass an OLD LANDING STRIP on the right, with its barrel-beacons still lying around. Twenty minutes later, turn inland on a SIGNPOSTED TRACK (**❷**; 40min). By now you may start feeling like Lawrence of Arabia and pining for a camel!

Clockwise from top left: Jandía lighthouse; Playa de Ojos; Jandía thistle (Euphorbia handiensis; *rock sorrel* (Rumex vesicarius) *sprouting up through thorny* aulaga; *Puertito de la Cruz, with its single wind turbine*

Five minutes later ignore a faint track off right; keep to the stone-lined trail. It loops slightly back and starts climbing towards the mountains. Magnificent views open up as you rise, especially at the HIGH POINT (❸; 1h20min).

Now start descending on a gravelly path rounding the hillside. The views are breathtaking, a just reward after your first hour in the desert. To the west is Punta Pesebre and towards the northeast you can see the arc of Cofete with the island's highest mountains — and even El Jable, an area covered with white-to-yellow sand made up mostly of particles of marine organisms.

Now you reach a LOW POINT with several dilapidated signposts above a spectacular coastline: **Água Cabras** (❹; 1h40min). On your right is a community of *tarajales* (tamarisks) in a small gully. On my last visit, these trees were still moist with dew at 11am, dripping water onto the ground for the goats to drink! Head south into the gully for a couple of hundred metres if you want to see some interesting petrified sand formations on the left. Then climb out on the right side of the gully, onto the waymarked track above. Follow it straight ahead for half an hour, until you cross the MAIN (SIGNPOSTED) TRACK TO PUERTITO.

Continue on to **Las Salinas** (❺; 2h20min), where a partly sandy beach invites you to take a dip. Climb the hill at the right of the beach and in an hour (joining the **GR 131**) you'll be back at **Puertito de la Cruz** (❻; 2h20min).

A day out on

Lanzarote

Car tour 4: A DAY OUT ON LANZAROTE — Playa Blanca • El Golfo • Yaiza • Parque Nacional de Timanfaya • Tinajo • La Santa • Monumento al Campesino • La Geria • Uga • Femés • Playa Blanca	116

WALKS ON LANZAROTE
31 Montaña Roja	124
32 The rock pools of Janubio	128
33 Punta de Papagayo	130
34 Atalaya de Femés	132
35 Degollada del Portugués	133

Touring map* *reverse of Fuerteventura touring map*

*The numbers on this touring map indicate car tours and walks in the book *Landscapes of Lanzarote*

Car tour 4: A DAY OUT ON LANZAROTE

Playa Blanca • El Golfo • Yaiza • Parque Nacional de Timanfaya • Tinajo • La Santa • Monumento al Campesino • La Geria • Uga • Femés • Playa Blanca

95km/59mi; 4 hours driving (plus 25-40 minutes on the ferry each way and any driving on Fuerteventura to reach Corralejo)
On route: Walks 31-35
*This is a **very** long day. **Do** plan on taking the first ferry in the morning and returning on the last one. There is no need to pre-book (outside the major holidays); just turn up about half an hour before sailing time and buy your tickets at the office on the pier in Corralejo. This tour takes in the south of Lanzarote — it's just not practicable to get to the north on a day trip from Fuerteventura, especially since you should allow at least an hour for your bus tour of the Timanfaya National Park and another half hour for the Visitors' Centre. To visit the famous Fámara cliffs or Jameos del in the north, you should spend at least one night on the island. Petrol stations are plentiful and roads are good, but be careful, some roads drop off sharply at the sides, into the vineyards or lava below — take special care here, as the scenery is so eye-catching that you could easily drive off the road. See map of Lanzarote on the reverse of the Fuerteventura touring map, and plan of Playa Blanca on pages 138-139.*

This route is short, but action-packed. You'll use up a whole day trying to fit everything in. And throughout the tour you'll be amazed at how the short ferry journey has taken you to a completely different world!

Car tour 4: A day out on Lanzarote

Referring to the plan on pages 138-139, head away from the port at Playa Blanca and turn right on the main road. At the roundabout (where the bus station, 'Estación de Guaguas' is to the left), turn left up to the next roundabout (⛽). Take the *third* exit from the roundabout, the LZ701 signposted for Yaiza. This old road runs parallel with the newer LZ2 'raceway' over to the right, zipping straight across the flat and featureless Rubicón Plain. Montaña Atalaya captures your attention on the right: on the way home you'll ascend high into its hidden valleys. The small village of Las Breñas, set back on a shelf off the plain, sits at the foot of Atalaya. Some 7km along, notice the isolated dark yellow building on the left; Walk 32 starts at this water desalination plant. The next eye-catcher is the salt pans, the **Salinas de Janubio**★ (📷), on the left. This basin of tiny rectangles reflects many tones of red, pink and orange in the intense sunlight.

Just beyond the salt pans, at 9.5km, you turn off for El Golfo. (Roundabout fever has caught on in Lanzarote, too.) Pass through **La Hoya** (📷✕), a few houses set back off the salt pans. Circling behind the pans, you get a clear view straight across them. A lagoon separates the salt pans from the black-sand beach of Playa de Janubio. Suddenly you're swallowed up in *malpaís* ('badland') lava. Superb sea views follow as you drive parallel with the coast. Several roadside parking bays allow you to pull over to enjoy the views (📷) of the low jagged and jutting lava sea-cliffs.

134 Landscapes of Fuerteventura

Then you come to the most famous outlook on this stretch of road, **Los Hervideros★** (☎; the 'boiling springs'), with a very large parking area. Here walkways have been carefully laid out through the maze of lava, where the waves pound into sea caves and you might get a soaking from some impressive blow-holes. Montaña Bermeja breaks the monochrome landscape with its rusty-red slopes.

Less than 2km further on, take the signposted turn-off left to the **Charco de Los Clicos★**, a cloudy green lagoon at the base of the El Golfo crater (photooverleaf). Then return to the main road and continue towards El Golfo. Circling behind the crater, turn left when you come to a junction. As the road descends, you'll see a parking area on the left *(not signposted)*, full of vehicles. This *mirador* affords an excellent view (☎) over the eroded **Golfo crater★**. This majestic, mostly-submarine volcano has been spectacularly eaten away by the sea, leaving one with the impression that it has been sliced in half. A path used to descend from here to the Charco de los Clicos, but it has been closed off to prevent erosion. From the viewpoint carry on down to the small seaside village of **El Golfo** (17km ✕), bustling with fish restaurants.

Return to the junction near the viewpoint and go left for Yaiza. Heading inland, volcanic mounds begin appearing. As you drive between two prominent cone-shaped hills, the ubiquitous Montaña Atalaya reappears. Passing under the LZ2, you join a roundabout, circle it and follow the *very small sign* indicating Yaiza. The road is lined with palms, aloes, and *tabaiba*. **Yaiza** (26km ♣✕🅿⊕) is neat, charming and spotless — manicured, in fact! The dark stone walls and *lapilli* fields make the white houses stand out even more. You pass the Iglesia de Los Remedios that stands in a square of the same name (photo overleaf).

Just past the church, turn left for the Montañas del Fuego. A junction follows: keep straight ahead through it. Passing under the LZ2 again, come to roundabout and go straight over. Soon you enter the **Parque Nacional de Timanfaya★** — announced by the symbol of the devil on the park's sign! Once again you're swallowed up by *malpais. (Note: you're not allowed to venture off the road while driving through the park.)* The island's showpiece, Pico Timanfaya, appears on the left. Both the mountain and the park take their name from the village of Timanfaya, which thrived in this rich agricultural area before being destroyed by six years of eruptions, beginning in 1730. The lichen-flecked lava gives the impression of sleet. It's an array of rich reds, browns, and charcoal. Further along more mounds ooze rust-brown. The turbulent landscape gives the impression you're experiencing the aftermath of a *recent* eruption.

If you fancy a ride on a camel, this is your chance, as you'll pass the **camel station★** on your left, 9km out of Yaiza. Even just watching the camel trains can be fun. Descending into a basin, you come to the park entrance (34.5km) and turn off left for the **Islote de Hilario** — departure point for the coach tours around the **Montañas del Fuego★**. An entrance fee, which includes the

Car tour 4: A day out on Lanzarote

tour, is paid here. After the park, your next stop should be the **Centro de Visitantes** (38.5km), with its excellent audio-visual show and exhibits. Farmlands follow, with fields of potatoes, onions, grapes, and low bushy fig trees.

Just outside the park boundary, **Mancha Blanca** (39.5km) sits on a crest overlooking the fields. Leaving the village, you come to a junction and bear left for Tinajo/La Santa. **Tinajo** (41km ♣✕☕) is an affluent farming town. Note the balconied Canarian homes. The town stretches out for some 3km: as you drive through it, keep right when the way forks. Heading straight over a roundabout, you cross an open barren plain. On this stretch of road, you'll encounter many cyclists in training from the La Santa sports complex. First you pass through the village of **La Santa** (47km ✕) and, 2km further on, you come to Club La Santa, a rather exclusive sports complex. It overlooks the rocky islet, La Isleta, and a pretty lagoon where all the wind-surfing takes place. To cross

Los Hervideros, with the rust-red slopes of Montaña Bermeja in the background

Church and square of Los Remedios in Yaiza (top), Charco de los Clicos (middle), and the half-moon stone walls protecting young vines in the lapilli *fields of La Geria (bottom)*

Car tour 4: A day out on Lanzarote

the *isleta*, curve left past the hotel reception and, when you come to a roundabout, keep right. Circle halfway round the islet; then, keeping the lagoon just to your left, cross the causeway and return to the main road.

Drive back to Tinajo and keep left on the LZ20 for San Bartolomé/Arrecife. **Tiagua** (61.5km ✕M), a typical farming village follows. In **Tao** (63km ✕📷) you experience a change in landscape. Grassy inclines begin appearing. Palms grace the village, which spreads over hillsides and hollows (photograph overleaf). Descending, you come into yet another small village, **Mozaga** (66km ✕🅿). Its fame rests on César Manrique's **Monumento al Campesino**★ at the large roundabout — make of it what you will.

Circling this roundabout, bear right on the LZ30 for **La Geria**★, the 'wine valley'. Aside from tourism, this is the most prosperous enterprise on the island. **Masdache** (68km ✕) is a well-dispersed village. From here on you'll pass several well-known *bodegas*. La Geria occupies a basin off the lava flow. The landscape here, pitted with hollows, is intriguing. The slopes are coated in black ash, and a myriad of low half-moon stone walls *(zocos)* edge the hollows and stretch across the countryside. This is the home of *malvasia* wine, the product of an ingenious farming method: the vines are planted in crater-like depressions layered with *lapilli,* which absorb moisture from the air and enable a single vine to produce as much as 200 kilos of grapes annually.

Crossing a crest, you descend to a junction (83.5km), with Montaña Atalaya staring straight at you. It overshadows **Uga** (✕), a sprawling village immediately over to your right. The LZ30 ends at a roundabout: go straight over, crossing the the LZ2, to begin the ascent to Femés (LZ702). This landscape, with its grassy hillsides, is more akin to the north of Lanzarote. Looking back, tremendous views of the inland hills unravel. Passing through the small village of **Las Casitas de Femés**, you ascend into a larger valley. Fields lie on either side of the road. **Femés** (88km ✕📷; Walks 34 and 35; photograph page 132) sits around the upper slopes of Montaña Atalaya. From the *mirador* in front of the church, the Balcón de Femés, you have a fine view over the Rubicón Plain to Playa Blanca, framed by the hills.

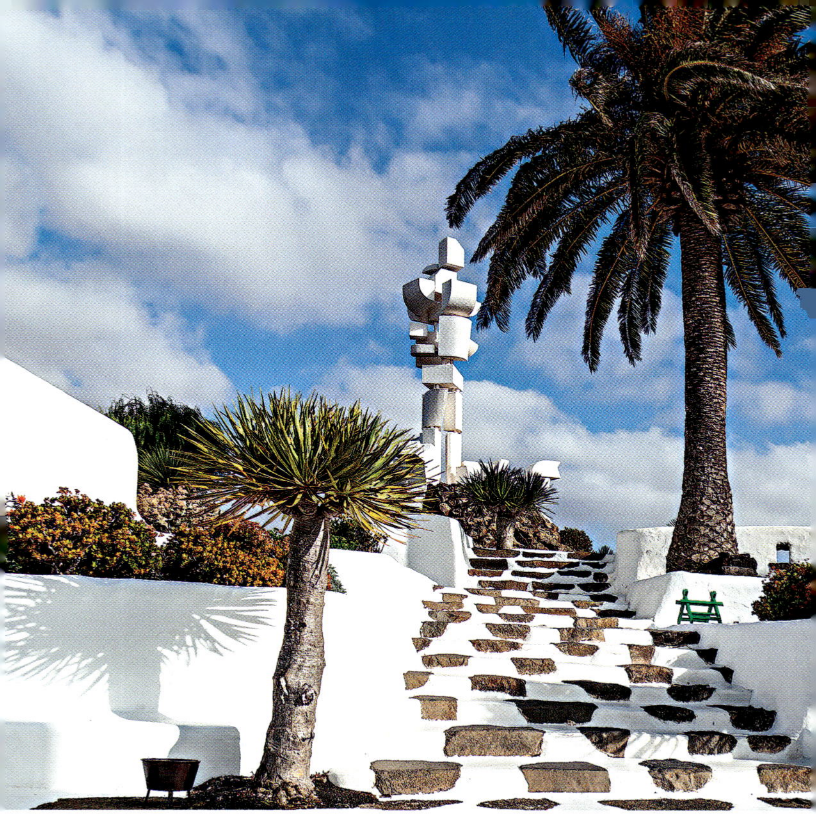

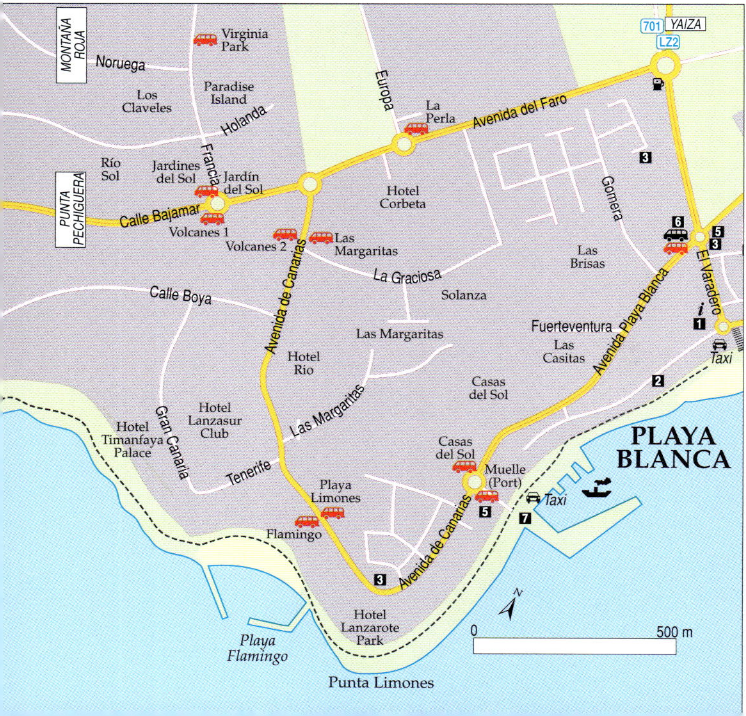

MONTAÑA ROJA
Virginia Park
Noruega
Paradise Island
Los Claveles
Holanda
Europa
La Perla
Avenida del Faro
701 YAIZA
LZ2
Río Sol
Jardines del Sol
Francia
Jardín del Sol
PUNTA PECHIGUERA
Calle Bajamar
Volcanes 1
Volcanes 2
Las Margaritas
Hotel Corbeta
Gomera
Las Brisas
El Varadero
La Graciosa
Solanza
Calle Boya
Avenida de Canarias
Las Margaritas
Fuerteventura
Las Casitas
Avenida Playa Blanca
Taxi
Hotel Rio
Casas del Sol
Hotel Lanzasur Club
Hotel Timanfaya Palace
Gran Canaria
Las Margaritas
Tenerife
PLAYA BLANCA
Casas del Sol
Muelle (Port)
Taxi
Playa Limones
Flamingo
Avenida de Canarias
Hotel Lanzarote Park
0
500 m
Playa Flamingo
Punta Limones

Above, left: the statue to Fecundity at the roundabout in Mozaga, seen from the Monumento al Campesino. As on Fuerteventura, artworks enliven roundabouts in Lanzarote; at the right is another of Manrique's creations.

At the roundabout below Femés, keep left for Playa Blanca, driving across the plain and straight over roundabouts. You come back to the roundabout by the bus station in **Playa Blanca**, from where the port is straight ahead.

If you're running earlier than expected, all the recommended leg-stretchers are close by: the two climbs from Femés (Walks 34 and 35), Walk 32 from the desalination plant, and a choice of two from Playa Blanca itself (Walks 31 and 33).

Walk 31: MONTAÑA ROJA

See map overleaf and town plan on pages 138-139
Distance: 3km/2mi; 1h05min
Grade: ● an easy climb/descent of 130m/425ft, but the volcanic pumice underfoot is slippery. No shade
Equipment: comfortable walking shoes with ankle support, fleece, sunhat, suncream, water
Transport: 🚗 to the roundabout with petrol station at the entrance to Playa Blanca, then turn right on the road to 'Faro de Pechiguera'. Pass the Elba Lanzarote Resort on the left in under 1km, go straight over the next roundabout and, at the *next* roundabout, turn right (sign: 'Jardines del Sol'). Pass the Jardines del Sol on the left, and when you are level with the Hotel Paradise Island on the right, turn left (Calle Noruega, signed to 'Montaña Baja, Los Claveles' among others. Keep ahead uphill for about 0.5km, then park in one of the streets below the easily-seen path up to a mobile phone mast and the crater (28° 52.179'N, 13° 50.905'W).

Montaña Roja is just a little pimple of a volcano, but in spring wonderful miniature gardens of wild flowers flourish in the pumice and, as the mountain rises in isolation on the Rubicón plain, it affords far-reaching views. At the end of your day out on Lanzarote, if you still have time before the last ferry, this short leg-stretcher will give you Lanzarote's finest views across to Fuerteventura and the sand dunes of Corralejo.

Walk 31: Montaña Roja 141

Start out by continuing uphill on Calle Noruega (there may be a sign *'TO THE VOLCANO'* here (**1**)). Then fork left to pass above Montaña Baja, heading for the mobile phone mast and the summit path.

It's only **15min** up to the RIM (**2**), where you can go either left or right. (Turn left if you're in a hurry, and you'll reach the trig point in only 10 minutes.) The main walk heads right, passing a *PATH INTO THE BOTTOM OF THE CRATER* (**3**), just 20m below. The crater floor is disfigured with 'graffiti' — small stones arranged to spell out the names of previous visitors.

As you round the basin, the urban sprawl and a network of roads comes into view — one leading to the large Atlante del Sol ruin in the northwest, an urbanization that was never completed. It stands isolated in a desert wilderness. In about **45min** or a little more you reach the high point of the walk at the **Montaña Roja** TRIG POINT (**4**; 194m), with a fine view down to the lighthouses at Pechiguera and over to Corralejo's dunes.

You'll be back at **2** in 10 minutes and down on Calle Noruega (**1**) in **1h05min**.

Rounding the small crater of Montaña Roja, you look down to the lighthouses at the Punta de Pechiguera. In the immediate surroundings are 'rock gardens', where delicate wild flowers flourish (top) and leaf-lichen (middle).

Walk 32: THE ROCK POOLS OF JANUBIO

See the map on pages 142-143
Distance: 8km/5mi; 2h20min
Grade: ● moderate; mostly level terrain underfoot, but you're floundering over uneven lava for much of the way. The descent to El Convento is vertiginous and dangerous if wet (but this may be omitted).
Equipment: stout shoes with grip or walking boots, sunhat, suncream, fleece, raingear, picnic, plenty of water, swimwear
Transport: 🚗 to/from the water desalination plant — a large isolated building off the FV701 (old road), 2.4km south of the El Golfo roundabout: start and end the walk there (28° 55.258'N, 13° 50.194'W); ample parking.

This coastal walk, with its superb unvisited rock pools, is an ideal leg-stretcher on a hot day. You follow a jagged, rocky coastline. There are no beaches, only natural rock pools — pools to suit all the family — hidden on the lava shelves that jut out into the sea. El Convento is an impressive sea cave you can visit en route.

Start the walk at the WATER DESALINATION PLANT (**O**): go down to the lava rocks near the shore and head left (southwest). About 10-15 minutes beyond the desalination plant you begin finding the best pools, so keep an eye out for them. The sea churns up against the shelf, replenishing these pools: obviously, swimming isn't recommended in bad weather or when the sea is rough.

At **10min**, from the edge of the plain, you'll spot a first sea-shelf with a number of pools embedded in it. A few minutes' scrambling over rocks and boulders brings you down to them. This is an excellent spot for children, but the pools are also deep enough for adults. Some eight minutes later, there is another vast shelf with more inviting pools. Finally, a few minutes past this spot, you will find a magnificent solitary pool. All of these emerald-green waterholes are simply irresistible…

Ten minutes after passing a STONE CROSS (**❶**) and a small PARKING AREA for jeep safaris, keep an eye out for a high round WHITE CONCRETE TRIG MARKER that stands on a point to your right. Here you scramble over all the rock, to the top of the cliffs at **Punta de Piedra Alta** (**❷**; **50min**), for a dramatic coastal overlook. Two

The rock pools near the water desalination plant are frequented by fishermen.

Walk 32: The rock pools of Janubio

inviting green pools lie in what appears to be — and for most people will be — an inaccessible shelf, immediately below. Behind the pools is an enormous cave — **El Convento** (❸)— with a 'cloistered' entrance opening back into the face of the cliff. A smaller cave sits to its right. Now the problem is: how to get there?

Absolutely sure-footed walkers could venture down to these pools and cave. I've not been down there for years. I found the safest way down was just beyond the second cave, some four to five minutes round the top of the cliff. I crossed some interesting rock formations, resembling large fragments of broken crockery. Straight off this area of rock, I dropped down onto 'lumps' of lava. Metres to the right (close to the edge of the cliff), a nose of rock revealed itself. *Make sure that breakers aren't crashing over the shelf,* and then descend *with care* to this superb, sheltered spot.

All fours are needed but, when the sea is calm, there is no danger.

The main walk leaves this tricky descent behind and continues along the coast for another 20 minutes — to the **Bufadero del Rincón del Palo** (❹; **1h15min**), a blowhole where the walk turns back. It's more noticeable for its noise than the spray of water. You'll find it on a sea-shelf set in the U of the next bay along (**Rincón del Palo**). The noise gives it away.

The return is much easier on the feet: you follow a track that lies just a few minutes back from the top of the cliff — slightly inland from the path. Heading back, you have a good view of the Golfo crater — the prominent orange-coloured cone rising up off the seashore. Remain on the track along the coast; ignore all turn-offs inland. By **2h20min** you should be back at the DESALINATION PLANT (⊙).

Walk 33: PUNTA DE PAPAGAYO

See the map on pages 142-143
Distance: 9km/5.6mi; 3h
Grade: ● easy, but there is no shade en route, and it can be very hot.
Equipment: comfortable walking shoes, fleece, sunhat, suncream, raingear, picnic, water, swimwear

Transport: 🚗 to/from the Castillo de las Coloradas, just east of Playa Blanca. (Or shorten the walk to 6km/3.7mi; 1h55min by driving *past* the Castillo de las Coloradas and parking north of the Sandos Papagayo Beach Resort: 28° 51.635'N, 13° 47.839'W)

If you would like to see 'how the other half lives', then head out to Punta de Papagayo and *Lanzarote's* finest beaches. After Sotavento de Jandía you are sure to be underwhelmed — but then Lanzarote is all about volcanoes, not *playas*...

Start off at the well-restored **Castillo de las Coloradas** (**0**; 1769; also called **Torre de Aguila**). Off this headland you have a good view back to Playa Blanca and towards the superb beaches scooped out of the open bay on your left which culminates in Punta de Papagayo.

The wide promenade rises and falls as it curves along the coast past several large apartment and hotel complexes. After crossing a BRIDGE, you come to **Playa de las Coloradas** (**❶**; also called Playa del Afe). This stony beach is the ugly duckling of the *playas*. Just past the beach the promenade ends in front of the SANDOS PAPAGAYO BEACH RESORT, from where a steep and skiddy path leads up to the headland.* Once at the top, you find a clear path over to Playa Mujeres. Low spiny *aulaga* is scattered across the plain. Wherever you find *aulaga*, there's usually *cosco* nearby. *Cosco* (the red ice plant shown on page 75) turns a vivid wine red in drought conditions, and great colonies of it stain the inclines. Its fruit was used to make a substitute *gofio* (normally a roasted corn flour), and was used as a thickening agent.

Some 35min into the walk the unsoilt **Playa Mujeres** is in sight (**❷**; **40min**) — the longest and widest of the Papagayo beaches. Casas del Papagayo, the only sign of civilisation out here, is the handful of buildings near the point. As you descend to the northern edge of the beach you will spot a tall LIME KILN built into the cliff and a BUNKER from the Spanish Civil War. Then, by a another BUNKER at the southern end of the beach, climb a sandy path along the top of the crest, dipping in and out of small *barrancos* which empty out into concealed coves below.

Playa del Pozo (**❸**; **55min**) is the next of the larger beaches. It takes its name from the 15th-century wells up to your left, the **Pozos de San Marcial del Rubicón** (**❹**). Their water, a mixture of rain off Los Ajaches and salt water seepage, was considered safe to drink — and

---

*This path is the 'traditional' route: everybody uses it. But if you don't fancy the scramble, walk back 400m and turn right just before the bridge, heading for the signposted commercial centre. Pass a parking area and, 150m from the seafront, bear right. Pick up a path between the commercial centre (right) and gardens (left). A walkers' sign indicates 'Playas Papagayo' along the road ahead. Follow the signs to the newer 'official' trail.

Walk 33: Punta de Papagayo

so the first European colonisers settled here.

From the southern end of Playa del Pozo the coastal path crosses another ridge. Now more enticing coves reveal themselves — like **Playa de la Cera**. Soon the old colonial settlement of Papagayo reappears ahead. Circling behind a couple of coves, you reach the top of the crest and the ruined **Casas del Papagayo** (**5**; **1h25min**), some of whichhave been done up to offer food and drink.

A rust-brown and deep mauve-coloured rocky promontory separates the two dazzling coves on either side of you. From here you have a striking view of the smooth-faced inland hills, as well as along the string of beaches you've just visited. Continue on the path curving round Playa de Papagayo. Below you is the beach and some tents fastened to the face of the hill. (If you find this path unnerving, just walk along the top of the crest. Soon meeting a track coming in from the left, follow it out to **Punta de Papagayo** (**6**; **1h35min**). Now Fuerteventura is very close, and Lobos stands out against the dunes of Corralejo.

Return the same way to the **Castillo de las Coloradas** (**0**; **3h**).

Playa de Papagayo and the Ajache hills

Walk 34: ATALAYA DE FEMÉS

See the map on pages 142-143
Distance: 3.2km/2mi; 1h30min
Grade: 🔴 fairly strenuous, but short, with an ascent/descent of 300m/1000ft
Equipment: stout shoes with good ankle support (or walking boots), warm jacket, sunhat, raingear, suncream, picnic, water
Transport: 🚌 to/from Femés; park near the bar (28° 54.786'N, 13° 46.765'W)

The view from the Atalaya de Femés is best appreciated at sunset and sunrise, when shadows creep across the countryside, and the last (or first) light captures the real beauty of Timanfaya and the Salinas de Janubio. As a day-visitor you will have to forego these pleasures, but sitting high above the village of Femés, you have the southern vista of Lanzarote all to yourself.

Start the walk facing BAR FEMÉS (🔴) on the main road: walk up the road at its left-hand side, keeping the church on your left. You will meet a brick-paved road: follow it uphill to the right. At the top of the road, where it bends right to rejoin the main road, take the concrete track up to the left (just in front of a green garage door). At the next junction, go straight ahead on asphalt. After 50m again go straight ahead on a track: follow this for 300m, then turn left up a track with a chain barrier.

At the **Atalaya de Femés** (🔴; 608m/1995ft; **50min**) a stupendous view unfolds. The remote (for this island!) little village of Femés lies straight below, huddled around the pass that descends to the Rubicón Plain. Fuerteventura and Lobos fill in the backdrop. And from up here you can almost count Timanfaya's colourful volcanoes. On the far side of the transmitter station, you look down onto Las Breñas, stretching along a raised shelf of cultivation above the Rubicón.

Return the same way to BAR FEMÉS (🔴; **1h30min**).

The pretty church square in Femés (top) and the view over Femés on the ascent to the Atalaya de Femés

Walk 35: DEGOLLADA DEL PORTUGUES

See the map on pages 142-143
Distance: 3.5km/2.2mi; 1h35min — or extend to a circuit (see text)
Grade: 🔵❗ fairly easy climb and descent of only 100m/330ft, but there is a possibility of vertigo on one stretch.
Equipment/Transport: as Walk 34 opposite

This very short foray to an attractive pass is an ideal leg-stretcher. If you have the time, however, you can extend it to one of my favourite circuits on Lanzarote — just follow the violet lines on the map to make a circular walk of 7.5km/4.7mi, 2h40min.

Start out at the ROUNDABOUT (⊙) on the main road in **Femés** by following the PR LZ 09 finger-posts up the tarred lane opposite BAR FEMES, making for some ugly concrete buildings seen ahead on the hilltop. The tarmac peters out, and you pass between two *aljibes* (❶; water tanks set into the ground). Walk just to the right of the main building, still on the road/track. Looking to the left now, the reason for this blot on the landscape reveals itself: there's the amusing sight of a GOAT FARM, and the large pen may be bursting with these delightful creatures.

The buildings lie at the edge of a crest, the **Loma del Pico de la Aceituna** (414m/1358ft; **10min**). From here you look down over the isolated **Barranco de la Higuera** — a huge abyss, lime green to gold in colour, due to the sparse sprinkling of grasses in the volcanic soil. Straight below you, the dry river bed traces an intricate meander in a pristine landscape.

Your ongoing path, the sign-posted **PR LZ 09**, is to your right, accompanied by a black pipe. Walk towards it, passing to the left of another building half sunken into the rock, and bearing slightly left downhill.

Crossing a SADDLE (❷) between **Pico de la Aceituna** and **Pico Redondo** (**30min**) you enjoy a fine view over the Rubicón Plain. By **40min** a new *barranco* drops away steeply to the right. Some people may find this stretch unnerving, but the path is amply wide. Five minutes later, go left at a fork, climbing the flanks of Pico Redondo to the **Degollada del Portugués** (❸; **47min**).

Then retrace your steps to **Femés** (⊙; **1h35min**).

Barrano de Higuera

BUS AND FERRY TIMETABLES

BUSES

The operator is Tiadhe: tel (34) 928 855 726; www.tiadhe.com. There are more services than those shown here. Be sure to pick up a current timetable when you arrive or check the web.

Line 01: Pto Rosario — Morro Jable (via Antigua, Tiscamanita, Gran Tarajal, Tarajalejo and Costa Calma); journey time approximately 2h15min
Departs Pto Rosario (Mon-Sat) 06.30-17.30, hourly on the half hour (except 18.30), then 19.00-21.00 hourly on the hour, and at 21.30; *(Sun, holidays)* 09.00, 11.00, 12.30, 13.30, 14.30, 15.00-21.00 hourly on the hour. *Departs Morro Jable (Mon-Fri)* 06.00, 8.00-13.00 hourly on the hour, 16.30, 17.00, 18.15, 19.00, 20.00, 22.30; *(Sat)* 07.00, 08.00, 09.30, 10.30, 11.00, 12.30, 14.00, 15.30, 16.30, 19.00, 22.30; *(Sun, holidays)* 08.00, 09.30, 10.30, 11.30, 12.30, 14.00, 15.30, 16.30, 17.00, 19.00, 22.30

Line 02: Puerto del Rosario — Vega de Río Palmas (via Tefía, Casillas del Angela, Llanos de la Concepción and Betancuria); journey time approximately 1h30min
Departs Pto Rosario (daily) 11.00, 14.30; *Departs Vega de Río Palmas (daily)* 12.30, 16.30

Line 03: Puerto del Rosario — Caleta de Fuste — Las Salinas; journey time approximately 25min *(Some buses start and end at Caleta de Fuste)*
Departs Pto Rosario (Mon-Sat) 06.30-22.00 every half hour (every 15min between 10.00 and 16.00); *(Sun)* 07.00-22.00 every hour; also 09.30, 12.30, 16.30, 18.30. *Departs Caleta de Fuste (Mon-Sat)* 07.00-22.00 every half hour (every 15min between 10.00 and 16.00); *(Sun)* 07.30-22.30 every hour; also 11.45, 14.45, 17.30, 18.45

Line 04: Pájara — Morro Jable (via Ajuy, Tuineje, Gran Tarajal and the coastal resorts); journey time approximately 2h15min
Departs Pájara daily at 06.15 and **Mon-Fri** at 10.30. *Departs Morro Jable daily* at 16.15

Line 05: Morro Jable — Costa Calma; journey time approximately 35min
Departs Morro Jable (Mon-Sat) 07.30-14.30 hourly on the half hour; *(Sun, holidays)* 09.30-13.30 hourly on the half hour. *Departs Costa Calma (Mon-Sat)* 08.30-15.30 hourly on the half hour; *(Sun, holidays)* 10.30-14.30 hourly on the half hour

Line 06: Puerto del Rosario — Corralejo; journey time approximately 50min
Departs Pto Rosario (Mon-Sat) 07.00-18.30 every half hour, then 19.00-23.00 every hour on the hour; *(Sun, holidays)* 07.00-22.00 hourly. *Departs Corralejo (Mon-Sat)* 06.00-18.00 every half hour (except 15.30), then 19.00, 20.00, 21.00, 22.00; *(Sun, holidays)* 07.00-22.00 hourly on the hour

Line 07: Puerto del Rosario — El Cotillo (via Tindaya, La Oliva and Lajares); journey time approximately 2h
Departs Pto Rosario daily 10.00, 14.15, 19.00. *Departs El Cotillo daily* 06.45, 12.00, 17.00

Line 08: Corralejo — El Cotillo (via Lajares and La Oliva); journey time about 50min
Departs Corralejo daily 09.00-21.00 every hour on the hour. *Departs El Cotillo daily* 8.00-20.00 every hour on the hour except for 14.00

Line 09: Pájara — Morro Jable (via Costa Calma); journey time approximately 2h15min
Departs Pájara daily 06.30. *Departs Morro Jable daily* 16.00.

Line 10 Pto Rosario — Morro Jable (via the airport, Caleta de Fuste, Las Salinas, Gran Tarajal and Costa Calma); journey time approximately 2h
Departs Pto Rosario (Mon-Sat) 9.00, 13.45, 16.00 (not Sat), 18.00; *(Sun)* 13.00, 18.00. *Departs Morro Jable (Mon-Sat)* 6.30, 11.30, 13.30 (not Sat), 15.45; *(Sun)* 09.00, 16.00

Line 111 Morro Jable to Punta de Jandía (via Cofete and Puertito de la Cruz)
Departs Morro Jable (daily) at 10.00 and 14.00; *departs Punta de Jandía 12.00, 16.00 (then goes on to Puertito de la Cruz and Cofete before heading to Morro Jable)*

FERRIES TO/FROM LOBOS (see www.navieranortour.com, ferryisladelobos.com)

There are three boats with up to six sailings a day from about 10.00 to 16.00 (18.00 in summer); the crossing takes some 20 minutes. 'El Majorero' is a glass-bottomed boat.

FERRIES BETWEEN CORRALEJO AND PLAYA BLANCA (LANZAROTE)

'Bocayna Express' and 'Buganvilla Express' (Fred Olsen Line; www.fredolsen.es); journey time 25min
Departs Corralejo daily from 06.15 to 19.00; *departs Playa Blanca daily* from 07.10 to 20.00. *Ferries depart approximately every hour, with a 2-3 hour break after 10.45/*

'Volcán de Tindaya' (Armas Line; www.naviera-armas.com); journey time 35min
Departs Corralejo daily (except Mon) from 07.45 to 20.00 approximately every two hours
Departs Playa Blanca daily (except Mon) from 06.45 to 19.00 approximately every two hours

Index

Geographical names comprise the only entries in this Index; for other entries, see Contents, page 3. **Bold-face type** indicates a photograph; *italic type* indicates a map. Both may be in addition to a text reference on the same page.

Água Cabras *127,* 128
Água de Bueyes 23, **36,** *85,* 87
Água Liques 106-7, 111, *112-3*
Ajuy 13, 18-9, 26, *90-1,* **92,** *92, 95,* 97, 150
Antigua 16, 21-3, 30, 77, *78,* **78-9,** 80, 87, 150
Arco de las Peñitas **90,** *90-1*
Aula de la Naturaleza Parra Medina *82,* **84**

Barranco
  de Ajuy *90-1, 92,* 94, *95*
  de Butihondo 19, *119, 122-3*
  de la Madre del Água *90-1,* **94-5,** *95*
  de la Peña *90-1, 92, 95,* **96**
  de las Peñitas 12, **13,** *17, 41,* 20, **88-9,** *90-1,* **91**
  de Pecenescal **110-1,** *112-3*
  de los Molinos 12, **70-1,** *71*
  del Convento **82,** *82*
  Gran Valle 25, 118-9, *120,* **121**
Bayuyo 36, 50, 53, *54-5,* 56
Betancuria 12, 16, 19, 21-2, 57, 77, *78,* 81, *82,* 83, 97, 150
Bimboy *99,* 100
Boca de Esquinzo *122-3,* 124

Caldera de Rebanada *54-5,* 56
Caldereta 34
Calderón Hondo 12, 36, 53, **54,** *54-5,* **55**
Caleta
  Beatriz 49, 52
  Negra 13, 19, 92-3, *95,* **96-7**
Caleta de Fuste 13-4, 30, 38, 98, *99,* 100, 150
  Plan *7*
Cañada de Melián *62-3,* **63**
Cardón **41**
Casa de los Coloneles **12,** 34, **35,** *64-5*
Casas de Gran Valle 119, *120*
Casas de Jorós 26
Casillas del Angel 9, 30, 66-7, *68-9,* 85
Cofete 13, 15, 25-6, 28-9, 93, 96, 117-9, *120,* **121,** 127-8, 150; *see also* Playa
  track to **15,** 26-7, **28**
Convento de San Buenaventura 12, 80-1, **82,** *82*
Corralejo 14, 30, 38, 44, 49-50, 53, *54-5,* **56,** 98, 150
  Dunes **32-3**
  Plan *10*

Cortijo de Cofete: *see* Villa Winter
Costa Calma 16-7, 38, 106, **108,** *108,* 109-10, *112-3,* 122, *125,* 126, 150

Degollada
  de Cofete 118, 119, *120,* **121**
  de Mojones 110, 111, *112-3*
  Degollada del Marrubio *78, 79,* 80, *82*

El Cotillo 10, 11, 30, 35, **38-9,** 49, **50-1,** 52, **58-9,** *59,* **60-1,** 62-3, 81, 150
El Jable **110-1,** *112-3*
El Roque **2,** 59, *62-3*
Embalse de los Molinos 33, 73, **74,** *74,* 75

Faro de la Entallada 23, **24**
Faro de El Tostón 11, 49, **50-1**
Fuente de Tababaire **40,** *64-5*
Fuentes de El Chupadero 57
Giniginamar 13, 23, 38, *102-3*
Gran Montaña *85,* **86,** 87, 89
Gran Tarajal 16, 23, 38, 150
  Plan *9*
Granadillos 20

Huertas de Chilegua 17

Jandía
  Lighthouse *127,* **128**
  Peninsula 16, 25-9, 110-49

La Alcogida 30, **31,** *68-9*
La Atalayita **101,** *101*
La Caldera (Lobos) 44, 46-7, **48**
La Lajita 24, 38
La Matilla 30-1, 33, **57,** *57*
La Oliva **4,** 9-10, **12,** 19, 30-1, 33-5, **40,** *64-5,* 150
La Pared (village, isthmus) 16-7, 38, 88, 105, **108,** 109, *112-3,* 150
Lajares 11, 35, **36,** 49-50, 52, 53, *54-5, 62-3,* 150
Lanzarote 130-50
  Atalaya de Femés 131, 133-4, *142-3,* 148
  Barranco de la Higuera *142-3,* **149**
  Bufadero del Rincón del Palo *142-3,* 144-5
  Castillo de las Coloradas *142-3,* 145-6
  Charco de Los Clicos 134, **136**
Lanzarote (continued)

Degollada del Portugués *142-3,* 149
El Convento *142-3,* 145
El Golfo 131-4, 144
El Rubicón *142-3*
Femés 131-2, 137, 139, *142-3,* **148,** 149
Islote de Hilario 134
Janubio 131, 133, *142-3,* **144-5,** 148
La Geria 131-2, **136-7**
La Hoya 133
La Santa 131-2, 135
Las Breñas 133, *142-3,* 148
Los Ajaches **56,** *142-3,* 146
Los Hervideros **135**
Mancha Blanca 135
Masdache 137
Montaña
  Atalaya 133, 134, 137
  Bermeja 134, **135**
  Roja **140-1,** *142-3*
Monumento al Campesino 105, 131-2, 137, **138-9**
Mozaga 137
Parque Nacional de Timanfaya 131, **132-3**
Playa
  de Janubio *126-7*
  de las Coloradas *126-7,* 130
  de Papagayo 46, *142-3,* 146, **147**
  del Pozo *126-7,* 131
  Mujeres *142-3,* 146
Playa Blanca 39, 46, **56,** 132-3, 137, 139-40, *142-3,* 146, 150
  Plan *138-9*
Punta
  de Pechiguera **140-1,** 142-3
Salinas de Janubio 148
Tao 137
Tiagua 137
Tinajo 131-2, 135, 137
Uga 131-2, 137, *142-3*
Yaiza 131-4, **136,** *142-3*
Las Parcelas 12, 31, 70, *71,* 72, 76
Las Playitas 16, **22,** 23, 38
Las Salinas 13, 98, *99,* **100,** 128, 150
Llanos de la Concepción 22, 33, 67, 69, 73, **74, 75,** 76, 150
Lobos 11, 30, 37, **44-5, 46-7,** *48,* 150
  Casas El Puertito 11, 44-5, *48*
  Faro de Martiño **46-7,** *48*
  Montaña La Caldera 44, 46, 47, **48,** *48*
  Playa de la Calera **44-5,** *48*
Los Boquetes **106-7,** *108,* 109, 111
Los Molinos *see* Puertito de Los Molinos

Majanicho 49-50, **51,** 53-4
Mirador
  de Morro Velosa 21, **80-1,** *82*
Mirador (continued)
  de Tababaire **40,** *64-5*
Montaña
  Arena **35**
  Bayuyo 36, 53, *54-5,* 56
  Cardón 17, 87, **104-5,** *105*
  Colorada **53,** *54-5*
  Frontón 12, 34, **35**
  Tindaya *64-5*
Morro Jable 14, 16-7, 23-6, **29,** 38, *116,* 118-22, 127, 150
  Plan *6*
Morro Janana *82,* **84**

Oasis Park 109

Pájara 1, 13, 16, **18-9,** 20, 150
Peña Horadada *92, 93, 95, 96*
Pico de la Zarza 16, 24, **114-5,** *116,* 117
Playa
  Barca *122-3*
  de Barlovento 13, 26, 28, 119
  de Águila *59,* 60
  de Butihondo 19, *119, 122-3*
  de Cofete **118-9,** *120,* **cover**
  de Esquinzo *59,* 61
  de Ojos 28, *127,* 128, **129**
  Playa de Sotavento 16, *122-3,* **124-5,** 126, 146
  Playa del Castillo **52, 58-9,** *59,* **60-1,** *62-3*
  Playa del Jurado *92,* 93, *95,* 96-7
Popcorn Beach **51**
Pozo Negro 30, 98, *99,* 101
Puertito de la Cruz) *127,* **128-9**
Puertito de Los Molinos 12, 30-1, 33, 67, **70-1,** *71, 72*
Puerto de la Torre *99,* **100**
Puerto del Rosario 9-10, 13, 22, 30
  Plan *8-9*
Punta de Jandía 25, 26, 28-9, 37, **128**
Punta Mallorquín *59*
Punta Pesebre 28, *127,* 128

Tarajalejo 23, 38, *102-3,* **103,** 104, 107, 150
Tefía 12, 31, 57, 66, **67, 68,** *68-9,* 150
Tegú 81
Tetir 30-1, 66, **67,** *68-9*
Tindaya 30, 33-4, 40, 57, *64-5,* 68, 150
Tiscamanita 16, 23, *85,* **86-7,** 150
Torre de El Tostón 58, *59,* **63**
Tuineje 23, 150

Vallebrón 30, 34, *64-5*
Valles de Ortega 23, **36**
Vega de Río Palmas 12, 16, **20-1, 24,** 69, 78, 80, *82,* 83-4, *85,* 86-9, *90-1,* 150
Villa Winter 25, **26-7,** 117-8, *120,* **121**
Vinamar 16, 115